THE POCKET IDIOT'S GUIDE TO

Beanie Babies

by Holly Stowe and Carol Turkington

alpha
books

A Division of Macmillan Reference USA
A Simon and Schuster Macmillan Company
1633 Broadway New York, NY 10019-6785

Copyright © 1998 Holly Stowe and Carol Turkington

International Standard Book Number: 0-02-863078-5
Library of Congress Catalog Card Number: 98-88317

01 00 99   8 7 6 5 4 3 2 1

Interpretation of the printing code: the rightmost number of the first series of numbers is the year of the book's printing; the rightmost number of the second series of numbers is the number of the book's printing. For example, a printing code of 99-1 shows that the first printing occurred in 1999.

Printed in the United States of America

Contents

Introduction

What do you get when you take about a square foot of plush fabric, some fiberfill stuffing, a bunch of small plastic beads, string, thread, paper, and a boatload of creative ideas combined with marketing genius? You get a national craze that's spreading world-wide: *Beanie Babies*.

There really is something magical about these toys, something that goes beyond the affordable retail price. They're well-made. They provoke the imagination. They're cuddly. They're non-violent. In short, they're a parent's dream toy!

Except it's not just kids who are flocking to the stores to stock up. Adults seem to melt when faced with the gentle charm of Humphrey the camel or the irresistible face of Smoochy the frog. Whole networks of Beanie mavens have sprouted up in villages, towns, and on the Internet. Yes, there are people who are "into" Beanies for purely financial interests, but true collectors share their passion openly and create bonds of friendship that carry on into other parts of their lives.

What You'll Find in This Book

The Pocket Idiot's Guide to Beanie Babies is your handy guide to checking out each and every individual Beanie Baby. You'll get the vital statistics: tag number, birthdate, retirement date, and a description of each Beanie. You'll also find photos of each and every Beanie. Unlike most other books, our Beanies are divided into groups by category (fish, dogs, cats, and so on).

And there's more! Numerous informational boxes in the margins provide extra nuggets of information:

Beanie Tails

In these boxes you'll find anecdotes and stories behind the Beanies that provide you with a little peek behind the scenes.

Baby Talk

If there's a term you don't understand in connection with Beanie Babies, look for the answer in these boxes.

On the Sly

The warnings in these boxes will help you become a more knowledgeable collector and help you avoid counterfeits and other mistakes that could cost you big money.

Get the Scoop

These boxes contain insider tips and hints to help you earn your B.B.A. (Bachelor's of Beanie Arts). This is where we provide you with all the extra details you never knew you didn't know!

Trademarks

Certain terms mentioned in this book that are known to be claimed as trademarks or service marks by the authors have been appropriately indicated. The authors and

About the Authors

Holly Stowe was sucked into the Beanie Baby vortex in the fall of 1996 when she was accosted by the fuzzy little critters while looking for a hospital gift for her father. Born in Chicago and raised in Northbrook, Illinois, not far from the Ty Mothership, she was a musician in a former life and has sung at both Carnegie Hall and the Kennedy Center. She turned to the Geek Side of the Force in the early '80s and made a career for herself as a computer systems analyst after yet a couple more college degrees in a vain attempt to decide what she wanted to be when she grew up.

Ms. Stowe is happily unmarried with three children, Winter, Chloe, and Yuno the Doofyboydog who share the house with four, no, make that eight as of early September, guinea pigs. She is not-quite-patiently waiting for a Beanie Baby German Shepherd Dog and Beanie Baby guinea pig.

In order to support her Beanie habit, Ms. Stowe has ruminated on the joys of Beanie Babies and Beanie collecting in *Beanie Collector,* for which she is a Contributing Editor, and has a regular column, "The Beanie Dance of Joy," in *Beanie Mania* Magazine that bespeaks of the human side of Beanies. She is also the author of the *Beanie Babies Collector's Guide* published by the editors of *Consumer*

Guide™ and is still trying to decide what she wants to be when she grows up.

Carol A. Turkington is the coauthor of *Managing Your Money the Lazy Way* and (with her husband G. Michael Kennedy) *Maintaining Your Car the Lazy Way.* She has written more than 25 other books and numerous magazine articles, and has personally tripped over each one of the more than 60 Beanie Babies in her daughter's private collection.

Chapter 1

Down by the Sea

From gnashing of felt teeth and nibbling of cloth seaweed to cracking of felt claws, the Beanie Baby sea creatures are a fearsome lot! Still, things can get confusing under the sea, where everybody tends to look alike. Whether it's Pinchers vs. Punchers, Echo vs. Flash, Digger vs. Digger (same Beanie, different colors!)—well, you can't tell the swimmers without a scorecard.

So pull up a beach chair, shake the sand out of your shoes, and read on about all the ins and outs of the world of underwater Beanie Babies.

Bubbles the Fish

- ➤ Style: 4078
- ➤ Birthday: 7-2-95
- ➤ Released: 6-3-95
- ➤ Retired: 5-11-97
- ➤ Hangtag: 3-4

Bubbles was part of the fish trio that included Coral and Goldie. Majestic in yellow and black stripes with yellow fins, she was retired in May 1997—but if you look around, you probably won't have any trouble reeling her in.

On the Sly

Things can get pretty fishy as Beanie values rise—so it should be no surprise that counterfeits of Bubbles exist. Before you buy, study her closely to make sure she's the real thing. (Counterfeit giveaway: uneven seams!)

Claude the Crab

- ➤ Style: 4083
- ➤ Birthday: 9-3-96
- ➤ Released: 5-11-97
- ➤ Retired:
- ➤ Hangtag: 4-5

This jewel-colored, tie-dyed crab has a cocky attitude, flashy on the outside with a cream-colored underbelly. Many collectors have more than one because they can't decide which of these beautiful Beanies they like best. If you're lucky, you'll be able to dig one of these collectibles out of the sand.

Get the Scoop

Claude's one-of-a-kind, tie-dyed plush makes each Beanie unique, so plop a few into your crab pots the first chance you get.

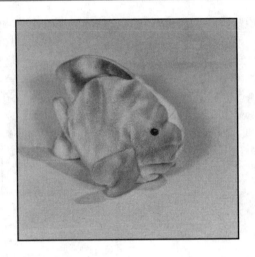

Coral the Fish

- ➤ Style: 4079
- ➤ Birthday: 3-2-95
- ➤ Released: 6-3-95
- ➤ Retired: 1-1-97
- ➤ Hangtag: 3-4

Coral is one of a shoal of Beanie fish (she shares a similar body type to both Bubbles and Goldie). Because of the tie-dyed method of plush coloration, her plushy scales range from muted to very bright. No matter where your Coral falls along the finny continuum, she'll be unique.

Get the Scoop

If you're convinced your Coral is looking a little squinty—one eye smaller than the other—you're not crazy! It's just that one eye is set more deeply into the plush.

Crunch the Shark

- ➤ Style: 4130
- ➤ Birthday: 1-13-96
- ➤ Released: 1-1-97
- ➤ Retired: 9-24-98
- ➤ Hangtag: 4-5

Long and skinny, Crunch's plush is steel blue (the same color as Echo the dolphin and Lefty the donkey) with a white underbelly. While the inside of his mouth is filled with red plush and lots of white teeth, don't worry! Crunch's teeth are felt.

Get the Scoop

Experts had been predicting Crunch was swimming toward retirement for quite some time (he was a bit of a slow seller).

Digger the Crab

- ➤ Style: 4027
- ➤ Birthday: (none) (orange)
- ➤ Birthday: 8-23-95 (red)
- ➤ Released: 6-25-94 (orange)
- ➤ Released: 6-3-95 (red)
- ➤ Retired: 6-3-95 (orange)
- ➤ Retired: 5-11-97 (red)
- ➤ Hangtag: 1-3 (orange)
- ➤ Hangtag: 3-4 (red)

Digger's original incarnation was bright all-orange, the same material as Chocolate's antlers and Caw's beak and feet. Sharing a body style with Claude, she was later redesigned with bright red plush. Don't get crabby if you have an orange Digger with the same style number—that's how they were produced.

Get the Scoop

While Digger comes in two colors, you'll find it easier to dig up the red version.

Echo the Dolphin

- ➤ Style: 4180
- ➤ Birthday: 12-21-96
- ➤ Released: 5-11-97
- ➤ Retired: 5-1-98
- ➤ Hangtag: 4-5

Like her name, Echo the dolphin isn't unique. She's simply an echo of Flash the dolphin. The first release was a bit schizophrenic: Her hang and tush tags said "Waves," and Waves' tags said "Echo." Her stomach and underside of her snout are white, and her back is the same steel blue as Crunch.

Get the Scoop

While she looks as graceful as any dolphin, Echo's is one of the more awkward Beanie styles; unless propped up, she tends to fall over on her steel blue back.

Flash the Dolphin

- ➤ Style: 4021
- ➤ Birthday: 5-13-93
- ➤ Released: 1-8-94
- ➤ Retired: 5-11-97
- ➤ Hangtag: 1-4

Flash and her counterpart Splash the whale were the first two of the Original Nine Beanies to be retired. Flash is light gray (like Righty and Manny) with a white underbelly.

Get the Scoop

In the "they could be twins" department: The white underbelly and lack of nostrils are the main features that distinguish Flash from the strikingly similar Manny the manatee.

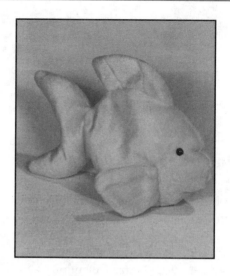

Goldie the Goldfish

- ➤ Style: 4023
- ➤ Birthday: 11-14-94
- ➤ Released: 6-25-94
- ➤ Retired: 12-31-97
- ➤ Hangtag: 1-4

Goldie, the last of the piscatorial Beanie trio to be retired, sports the bright orange plush seen on Scoop's beak and feet. Her dorsal fin is more pointed than Bubbles' and Coral's, and her tail is split into a wide V-shape.

Get the Scoop

While Goldie was the last of the fish trio to be flushed away to retirement, she was the first of her fishy friends to be released.

Inky the Octopus

- ➤ Style: 4028
- ➤ Birthday: (none) (tan—no mouth)
- ➤ Birthday: (none) (tan—mouth)
- ➤ Birthday: 11-29-94 (pink)
- ➤ Released: 6-25-94 (tan—no mouth)
- ➤ Released: 9-12-94 (tan—mouth)
- ➤ Released: 6-3-95 (pink)
- ➤ Retired: 9-12-94 (tan—no mouth)
- ➤ Retired: 6-3-95 (tan—mouth)
- ➤ Retired: 5-1-98 (pink)
- ➤ Hangtag: 1-2 (tan—no mouth)
- ➤ Hangtag: 3 (tan—mouth)
- ➤ Hangtag: 3-5 (pink)

Inky is one of only seven Beanies to have gone through three different designs. The original Inky was a fine taupe with black-on-white eyes and no mouth. In his next incarnation, he had that same dull taupe. He also appeared with a thread mouth sewn under the eyes. Eventually, Ty got the message and replaced the duller taupe with a jazzier pink tone. The thread mouth stayed.

On the Sly

Check to make sure Inky's eyes aren't all scratched up and that the stitching for the mouth wasn't removed by hand.

Jolly the Walrus

- ➤ Style: 4082
- ➤ Birthday: 12-2-96
- ➤ Released: 5-11-97
- ➤ Retired: 5-1-98
- ➤ Hangtag: 4-5

On the blazing Halley's Comet Scale of "cute," Jolly definitely scores higher than Tusk the walrus, whom he replaced. However, Jolly has the same design problem as co-releases Echo and Waves: He has no backbone! He doesn't sit up very well on his own, and if he's not propped up, you can expect him to roll over. He's covered in brown plush, but his most notable feature (besides his tusks) is his extremely fuzzy mustache.

Get the Scoop

If you're frustrated with your wobbly walrus, think about displaying him in a clear acrylic display box. He'll be guaranteed to sit up straight!

Legs the Frog

- ➤ Style: 4020
- ➤ Birthday: 4-25-93
- ➤ Released: 1-8-94
- ➤ Retired: 10-1-97
- ➤ Hangtag: 1-4

An amphibian in the true Shaker style and one of the Original Nine Beanies, Legs is one of the plainest critters Ty makes. With the same medium-green plush that he shares with Speedy the turtle, he lacks any distinguishing features other than his eyes.

Get the Scoop

Earlier versions of Legs with swing tags are hard to come by, but the later tagged versions are as plentiful as june bugs on a lily pond—and still inexpensive.

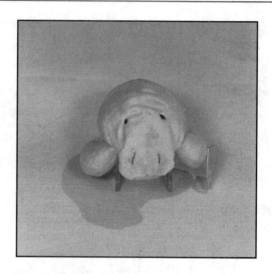

Manny the Manatee

- ➤ Style: 4081
- ➤ Birthday: 6-8-95
- ➤ Released: 1-7-96
- ➤ Retired: 5-11-97
- ➤ Hangtag: 3-4

No, you're not seeing double: Manny's shape and light gray plush are often confused with Flash the dolphin. Here's the difference: Manny has embroidered nostrils and a more rounded nose—and she lacks Flash's white stomach.

Get the Scoop

Manny's unpopularity on store shelves (she was an all-time sluggish seller) has helped boost her value since she retired.

Patti the Platypus

- ➤ Style: 4025
- ➤ Birthday: (none) (maroon)
- ➤ Birthday: 1-6-93 (fuchsia)
- ➤ Released: 1-8-94 (maroon)
- ➤ Released: 2-28-95 (fuchsia)
- ➤ Retired: 2-28-97 (maroon)
- ➤ Retired: 5-1-98 (fuchsia)
- ➤ Hangtag: 1-3 (maroon)
- ➤ Hangtag: 3-5 (fuchsia)

Call her "Patti the Flatty"—she's one of the flattest Bean-ies—and no matter how many times she's redesigned in different shades, she's consistently rolled off the conveyor belt with the same wide gold beak and "paddles." She comes in at least two different colors of plush: First came maroon, and then came fuchsia (also referred to as purple, orchid, or magenta).

Get the Scoop

Patti may come in as many as four colors, but some of the subtle varia-tions may be the result of dye lot differences in the fabric.

Pinchers/Punchers the Lobster

- ➤ Style: 4026
- ➤ Birthday: 6-19-93
- ➤ Released: 1-8-94 (Pinchers)
- ➤ Released: 1993 (Punchers)
- ➤ Retired: 5-1-98 (Pinchers)
- ➤ Retired: (pre-Beanies) (Punchers)
- ➤ Hangtag: 2-5 (Pinchers)
- ➤ Hangtag: 1 (Punchers)

The bright red Pinchers was one of the Original Nine Beanies released in January 1994. He has two black string whiskers of uneven length (either very long or very short). The difference between Pinchers and his earlier *pre-Beanie* version, Punchers, is in the spacing of the segments of the tail: The two inner segments on Pinchers are more narrow than the two outer segments.

Get the Scoop

The difference between Punchers and Pinchers is so slight that most people insist on checking Punchers' hangtag to prove his identity.

Seamore the Seal

- ➤ Style: 4029
- ➤ Birthday: 12-14-96
- ➤ Released: 6-25-94
- ➤ Retired: 10-1-97
- ➤ Hangtag: 1-4

Seamore is all white plush with a black plastic nose and whiskers and embroidered eyebrows. She was hard to find in stores before her October 1997 retirement, and afterwards her value briefly skyrocketed.

Get the Scoop

Seamore is the most valuable Beanie from the October 1997 retirement group. Finding a mint condition Seamore is harder than balancing a beach ball on the end of your nose; but if you do, hang on to her!

Seaweed the Otter

- ➤ Style: 4080
- ➤ Birthday: 3-19-96
- ➤ Released: 1-7-96
- ➤ Retired: 9-19-98
- ➤ Hangtag: 3-5

Unlike some of the floppier Beanie sea creatures, Seaweed's tail helps her maintain a sitting position—but she can also lie on her back just like real otters, who spend a great deal of time floating around this way. Seaweed has dark brown plush with a medium brown plush snout. Missing from action for the last couple months before her retirement, her value "otter" go up fairly quickly.

Get the Scoop

Only a few Beanies boast felt as a decoration; Seaweed is one of them! A vegetarian, as are all good otters, she nibbles a tasty morsel of green felt seaweed in her paws.

Splash the Whale

- ➤ Style: 4022
- ➤ Birthday: 7-8-93
- ➤ Released: 1-8-94
- ➤ Retired: 5-11-97
- ➤ Hangtag: 1-4

Splash and his fraternal twin Flash were among the Original Nine Beanies, both of whom were retired in May 1997, and replaced with the moderately short-lived Waves and Echo. Splash has beautiful black plush on his back and fins, but his underbelly, like all proper Orca whales, is white.

Get the Scoop

Thar he blows! Some people think Splash is a tad more rare than Flash, his twin, but others don't believe it makes a whale of a difference. They are both good value if you can harpoon one.

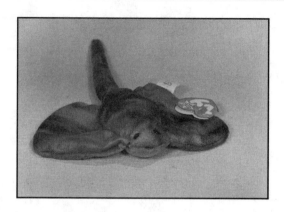

Sting the Stingray

- ➤ Style: 4077
- ➤ Birthday: 8-27-95
- ➤ Released: 6-3-95
- ➤ Retired: 1-1-97
- ➤ Hangtag: 3-4

Sting and Bronty share the same deep blue, tie-dyed plush, but it seems far more appropriate to this beautiful sea creature. Who ever heard of a blue brontosaurus, anyway? Initial introduction photos of this guy sported a white belly, but he's been all blue up to his retirement New Year's Day 1997.

On the Sly

Beware! All those "beans" in Sting's tail can make it hard to bend, which can lead to some popped stitches where the tail connects to his body.

Tusk the Walrus

- ➤ Style: 4076
- ➤ Birthday: 9-18-95
- ➤ Released: 1-7-95
- ➤ Retired: 1-1-97
- ➤ Hangtag: 3-4

Much plainer than his toothy descendant Jolly the walrus, Tusk has brown plush over all but his snout, which is a lighter brown. His white felt tusks can face either forward or backward. Notice that Ty often uses the Beanies' poems to drive home an educational point to their younger customers.

Get the Scoop

Some of the later versions of Tusk had a hangtag with his name spelled "Tuck"—this error makes him slightly more valuable, despite being a poor speller.

Waddle the Penguin

- ➤ Style: 4075
- ➤ Birthday: 12-19-95
- ➤ Released: 6-3-95
- ➤ Retired: 5-1-98
- ➤ Hangtag: 3-5

He's a fat and sassy fellow, dressed in formal attire: black plush on his head, back, and the top of his wings. The underside of his wings and his belly are white plush. His beak and feet are bright orange and his "bow tie" is bright yellow plush. Waddle on over to your nearest store, where you may still find him on the shelves.

Get the Scoop

Although Waddle was reincarnated in midget form as one of the 1998 Teenie Beanies, full-sized Waddle was retired before his release in miniature.

Waves the Whale

- ➤ Style: 4084
- ➤ Birthday: 12-8-96
- ➤ Released: 5-11-97
- ➤ Retired: 5-1-98
- ➤ Hangtag: 4-5

Waves was never as popular (or easy to display) as his predecessor Splash. It was a whale of a mixup as the first shipments of Waves arrived in the stores bearing Echo's hang- and tush tags (and vice versa).

Get the Scoop

The mistagged Waves and Echo are now worth slightly more than the correctly tagged versions, though neither is very expensive.

Chapter 2

Here Kitty, Kitty...

Have trouble telling the Zips from the Chips, the Nips from the Snips? You're not alone! We're here to get this all straight for you, once and for all.

In this chapter, you'll find the lowdown on all the Beanie Baby cats. For convenience's sake (and because the "wildlife" chapter was already filled to overflowing) we've also included the wild cats in this group—so look here for Blizzard the tiger, Freckles the leopard, and Stripes the tiger.

Blizzard the Tiger

- ➤ Style: 4163
- ➤ Birthday: 12-12-96
- ➤ Released: 5-11-97
- ➤ Retired: 5-1-98
- ➤ Hangtag: 4-5

You might expect her to be pure white, but Blizzard has black stripes on that white body. You can tell the difference between her and Ziggy the zebra by measuring the stripes: Blizzard's are farther apart. With her pink nose, black whiskers, and blue eyes, she has been an extremely popular member of the leopard-tiger-panther group.

Get the Scoop

Rumors of retirement due to trademark claims (Dairy Queen already had a "Blizzard" frozen treat) followed her from the time of her release up until the day she was retired. In case you wondered: No, the rumors weren't true.

Chip the Cat

- ➤ Style: 4121
- ➤ Birthday: 1-26-96
- ➤ Released: 5-1-97
- ➤ Retired:
- ➤ Hangtag: 4-5

Chip looks like a Frankenstein version of Nip and Zip, with two-thirds of her face and one ear gold plush, and the other side and ear black. Her paws and the inside of her ears are white, and she's got a pink nose and white whiskers. Chip was a very popular addition to the Beanie cats, which include Flip, Nip, Snip, and Zip.

Get the Scoop

You won't find huge piles of Chips at your local store, but if you search you may still uncover some.

Flip the White Cat

- ➤ Style: 4012
- ➤ Birthday: 2-28-95
- ➤ Released: 1-7-96
- ➤ Retired: 10-1-97
- ➤ Hangtag: 3-4

All bets were off (which cat would be retired first?) as Flip went sailing into retirement, the first of the Beanie cats to do so. All white with a pink nose and whiskers, her interior ears are pink plush as well.

On the Sly

Flip's baby blues are a standout, but like all white Beanies, Flip can be a pain to keep clean!

Freckles the Leopard

➤ Style: 4066
➤ Birthday: 6-3-96
➤ Released: 6-15-96
➤ Retired:
➤ Hangtag: 4-5

Freckles is—well, freckled all over with leopard spots, but he's shaped like his cousins Stripes the tiger and Velvet the panther (both now retired). Pink-nosed and black-whiskered, his tail comes in two varieties: flat with visible stitching or round with hidden stitching.

Get the Scoop

Freckles' unusual plush design has had collectors clamoring for more; he's usually one of the first to get snapped up from store shelves.

Nip the Cat

- ➤ Style: 4003
- ➤ Birthday: (none) (white face)
- ➤ Birthday: (none) (all gold)
- ➤ Birthday: 3-6-94 (white paws)
- ➤ Released: 1-7-95 (white face)
- ➤ Released: 1-7-96 (all gold)
- ➤ Released: 3-10-96 (white paws)
- ➤ Retired: 1-7-96 (white face)
- ➤ Retired: 3-10-96 (all gold)
- ➤ Retired: 12-31-97 (white paws)
- ➤ Hangtag: 2-3 (white face)
- ➤ Hangtag: 3 (all gold)
- ➤ Hangtag: 3-4 (white paws)

Another three-variation Beanie, Nip was first released with a very round face, pink inner ears, and a white plush triangle that extended over his belly. In his second incarnation, he appeared with a smaller, more triangular-shaped face in all gold (except for the pink in his ears). Both these first two versions had pink plastic noses and pink string whiskers. In his third appearance, he kept his all-gold plush but now sports white paws and white inner ears. The pink string whiskers turned white.

Get the Scoop

The second variation of Nip is the hardest to get.

Pounce the Cat

- ➤ Style: 4122
- ➤ Birthday: 8-28-97
- ➤ Released: 12-31-97
- ➤ Retired:
- ➤ Hangtag: 5

When Pounce was first released, her tie-dyed brown plush was a fabric innovation. Many people thought there was something wrong with their Pounce, since the fabric wasn't an even color. (The tie-dye variations are very subtle.) Her paws, inner ears, and chin are off-white, and she has a pink nose and mouth and brown string whiskers.

Get the Scoop

No, Pounce is not going to be recalled because her name is the same as a popular cat treat—that's just a rumor!

Prance the Cat

- ➤ Style: 4123
- ➤ Birthday: 11-20-97
- ➤ Released: 12-31-97
- ➤ Retired:
- ➤ Hangtag: 5

The black-on-gray striped plush on Prance is a first for the Beanie line; her paws and inner ears are white, and she has a white spot on her forehead. Blue eyes and a pink nose, mouth, and whiskers complete the package.

Get the Scoop

Can't keep Pounce and Prance straight? Try remembering that alphabetically, brown comes before gray, so Pounce comes before Prance.

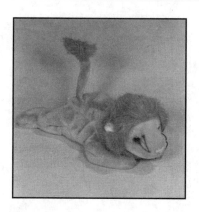

Roary the Lion

- ➤ Style: 4069
- ➤ Birthday: 2-20-96
- ➤ Released: 5-11-97
- ➤ Retired:
- ➤ Hangtag: 4-5

Roary borrowed the fake fur from Nuts the squirrel's tail in order to have a full mane and a ball of fur on the tip of his tail. Covered in brown plush, his inner ears and chin are off-white. He has black whiskers, but shares his small fuzzy plastic nose with Velvet the panther.

Get the Scoop

If you've got young friends, you know that Roary is a particular favorite of youngsters (perhaps because of Disney's *The Lion King*).

Snip the Siamese Cat

- ➤ Style: 4120
- ➤ Birthday: 10-22-96
- ➤ Released: 1-1-97
- ➤ Retired:
- ➤ Hangtag: 4-5

Just as you'd expect from a Siamese, Snip has big blue eyes, cream-colored plush fur, and brown points on each paw, the tip of her tail, her inner ears, and her face just above her nose. The nose is black plastic, with dark brown whiskers.

Get the Scoop

While there are more dog Beanies than there are cats at the moment, you feline aficionados can count on more cat breeds being born in the next two years to even the score.

Stripes the Tiger

- ➤ Style: 4065
- ➤ Birthday: (none) (dark)
- ➤ Birthday: 6-11-95 (light)
- ➤ Released: 1-7-96 (dark)
- ➤ Released: 6-3-96 (light)
- ➤ Retired: 6-3-96 (dark)
- ➤ Retired: 5-1-98 (light)
- ➤ Hangtag: 3 (dark)
- ➤ Hangtag: 4-5 (light)

Dark stripes/light stripes, old stripes/new stripes, thin stripes/fat stripes...if it's stripes you want, you can get 'em all in various Beanie Babies, all variations on the tiger theme. The older Stripes has black stripes on dark-gold material, while the newer, more common version has fewer black stripes on a yellow-tan plush. Both have fuzzy pink plastic noses and black whiskers.

Get the Scoop

If you're into collecting, try to bag the rare version of the darker Stripes with fuzzier material on the belly. It's worth significantly more money.

Velvet the Panther

- ➤ Style: 4064
- ➤ Birthday: 12-16-95
- ➤ Released: 6-3-95
- ➤ Retired: 10-1-97
- ➤ Hangtag: 3-4

This beautiful black plush panther's most distinguishing feature is her fuzzy pink plastic nose found on many of the Beanie cats, both wild and domestic. (Those of you who like realism in your wild cats will be pleased with these details: You can even see the nostrils.)

Get the Scoop

Velvet comes in both round- and flat-tailed versions, but they're all worth the same.

Zip the Cat

- ➤ Style: 4004
- ➤ Birthday: (none) (white face)
- ➤ Birthday: (none) (all black)
- ➤ Birthday: 3-28-94 (white paws)
- ➤ Released: 1-7-95 (white face)
- ➤ Released: 1-7-96 (all black)
- ➤ Released: 3-10-96 (white paws)
- ➤ Retired: 1-7-96 (white face)
- ➤ Retired: 3-10-96 (all black)
- ➤ Retired: 12-31-97 (white paws)
- ➤ Hangtag: 2-3 (white face)
- ➤ Hangtag: 3 (all black)
- ➤ Hangtag: 3-4 (white paws)

Zip the cat, like his pal Nip, has worked his way through three variations of his nine lives. In his first life, he was born with a face as round as a pumpkin, with a triangle of white plush from the middle of his forehead extending under his chin and over his belly. The second and most rare (rarer than the all-gold Nip) variation is all black. Both versions come with pink inner ears, pink plastic noses, and pink string whiskers. The final variation has white inner ears, whiskers, and paws, and is the hardest to find among all the May 1998 retirees. All three Zips have green eyes.

Get the Scoop

The second-edition Zip (all black) is even rarer than the all-gold Nip. If you've got this one stashed in your collection, break out the catnip and celebrate!

Chapter 3

Old McDonald Had a Farm

In This Chapter

➤ Learn how to tell the Beanie bunnies apart

➤ Find out which Beanie hit the sauce and got renamed

➤ Read all about a cow with a gender identity problem

If you live on a farm—or just dream of living the rural life—you'll find plenty of cuddly Ty Beanies to fulfill your country aspirations. In this chapter, we outline all you need to know about each one.

While you'll find all the traditional farm creatures here, you'll also find all of the rabbits, too. While technically "wild" critters, they are often raised on farms and seemed to fit in well with their fellow barn Beanies.

Bessie the Cow

- ➤ Style: 4009
- ➤ Birthday: 6-27-95
- ➤ Released: 6-3-95
- ➤ Retired: 10-1-97
- ➤ Hangtag: 2-4

Bessie is a brown and white "sit-up" style cow who was a companion to Daisy, the black and white "lay-down" cow, until Bessie got put out to pasture last October 1. Daisy followed just two weeks shy of a year later, having retired on September 15, 1998.

Get the Scoop
She's udderly divine, but why does this lady cow have horns?

Chops the Lamb

- ➤ Style: 4019
- ➤ Birthday: 5-3-96
- ➤ Released: 1-7-96
- ➤ Retired: 1-1-97
- ➤ Hangtag: 3-4

If you're counting sheep, Chops was the first of two Beanie ovines (Fleece was the other) to hit the market. Chops has cream-colored plush with a black face and black interior ears, and a pink nose.

Get the Scoop

It was rumored that Chops was retired (way too early, many say!) due to a name conflict with the late Shari Lewis' puppet, Lamb Chop.

Daisy the Cow

- ➤ Style: 4006
- ➤ Birthday: 5-10-94
- ➤ Released: 6-25-94
- ➤ Retired: 9-15-98
- ➤ Hangtag: 1-5

Daisy is a lay-down cow, unlike her similarly retired bovine sister, Bessie. Mostly black with a broad white stripe down her face and white inner ears, Daisy also sports a white spot on the left side of her back and has light tan horns.

Get the Scoop

Daisy sported a special hangtag for the Chicago Cubs in memory of legendary broadcaster Harry Caray as part of a promotion.

Derby the Horse

- ➤ Style: 4008
- ➤ Birthday: (none) (fine-mane)
- ➤ Birthday: 9-16-95 (coarse-mane)
- ➤ Birthday: 9-16-95 (star)
- ➤ Release: 6-3-95 (fine-mane)
- ➤ Release: (unknown) (coarse-mane)
- ➤ Release: 12-15-97 (star)
- ➤ Retired: (unknown) (fine-mane)
- ➤ Retired: 12-15-97 (coarse-mane)
- ➤ Retired: (star)
- ➤ Hangtag: 3 (fine-mane)
- ➤ Hangtag: 3-4 (coarse-mane)
- ➤ Hangtag: 5 (star)

Derby is one of the few Beanies who have undergone two design changes. In his initial entry into the Ty stable, he came equipped with a mane and tail of fine brown yarn to contrast his lighter-brown plush. The fine yarn gave way to thicker, coarser brown yarn, and then at the start of 1998, Derby earned a white star on his forehead.

Get the Scoop

The fine-maned Derby version is very rare, so if you want this one you'll have to pony up quite a bit of spare change.

Doodle the Rooster (now Strut)

➤ Style: 4171
➤ Birthday: 3-8-96
➤ Released: 5-11-97
➤ Retired: 7-12-97 (Doodle)
➤ Retired: (Strut)
➤ Hangtag: 4

Doodle wasn't long for the Beanie world when he was retired due to a name conflict. (There was already a "Doodles" chicken—the mascot of restaurant chain Chick-Fil-A.) This Beanie rooster is no chicken: He's colorfully made of pink, magenta, yellow, and green tie-dye with long yellow legs and beak. His wings and tail are bright red plush to match his felt comb and waddle. He was not redesigned after the renaming.

Get the Scoop

Doodles was distributed on a limited basis. Once news of his new name dribbled out, his worth skyrocketed from $10 to more than $100!

Ears the Brown Rabbit

- ➤ Style: 4018
- ➤ Birthday: 4-18-95
- ➤ Released: 1-7-96
- ➤ Retired: 5-1-98
- ➤ Hangtag: 3-5

Ears was the first and most realistic of the Beanie rabbits, since he's designed to stretch out just like living, breathing lagomorphs. Brown with a cute white tail, the insides of his long ears and his mouth are also white, and he has pink string whiskers and nose. He retired along with his three pastel compatriots in May 1998, but should still be easy to find.

Get the Scoop

If you're looking for a unique way to decorate your home for the Easter holidays, what could be more festive than little brown Ears peeking out of a spring flower arrangement?

Fleece the Lamb

- ➤ Style: 4125
- ➤ Birthday: 3-21-96
- ➤ Released: 1-1-97
- ➤ Retired:
- ➤ Hangtag: 4-5

Fleece is as white as snow (at least, she is when she's new!), but her plush is unique among most Beanies in that it's nappy rather than smooth. The sweet-faced replacement for Chops, the black-faced lamb, Fleece has a cream-colored face and small pink nose.

On the Sly

Be careful of how you display Fleece; her fur can quickly mutate from white as snow to dull as dishwater if you're not careful.

Floppity the Lilac Bunny

- ➤ Style: 4118
- ➤ Birthday: 5-28-96
- ➤ Released: 1-1-97
- ➤ Retired: 5-1-98
- ➤ Hangtag: 4-5

Lovely light-lilac, Floppity is one of a trio of pastel bunnies as pretty as a row of Easter eggs on a spring morning. (Hippity and Hoppity are the other two.) Floppity has a pink nose, whiskers, and pink plush under the ears. A totally color-coordinated bunny, she has a lavender bow that matches her plush.

Get the Scoop

Have trouble remembering which bunny is which color? Put the colors in alphabetical order—lilac, mint, and rose—and you have the order of their names, too.

Gobbles the Turkey

➤ Style: 4023
➤ Birthday: 11-27-96
➤ Released: 10-1-97
➤ Retired:
➤ Hangtag: 4-5

Gobbles is decorated in harvest colors of red, yellow, brown, and white. Her head is red with a yellow beak. Yellow is also found under her wings and on her feet. She has a red felt waddle and two embroidered nostrils. Her body and the base of her tail are brown plush with a middle arc of red and outer arc of white. She is a large, impressive Beanie—quite beautiful when her tail is fanned out.

Get the Scoop

Having a Thanksgiving dinner and stumped for party favors for the kids' table? Look no further. Gregarious Gobbles will be a sure-fire holiday hit!

Hippity the Mint Bunny

- ➤ Style: 4119
- ➤ Birthday: 6-1-96
- ➤ Released: 1-1-97
- ➤ Retired: 5-1-98
- ➤ Hangtag: 4-5

The middle of the bunny trio of Floppity, Hippity, and Hoppity, Hippity is a medium mint-green with a matching ribbon around his neck. He has a pink nose and whiskers, and the undersides of his long ears are pink as well.

Get the Scoop

Hippity is usually considered the most difficult of the three pastel bunnies to dig up. If you find him, hop right out and snap him up!

Hoppity the Rose Bunny

➤ Style: 4117
➤ Birthday: 4-3-96
➤ Released: 1-1-97
➤ Retired: 5-1-98
➤ Hangtag: 4-5

This little bunny is all pink, from the tip of her nose down to her toes. Like her buddies Floppity and Hippity, the undersides of her ears are pink, but with her coloring you don't notice. Like the other bunnies, Hoppity's ribbon around her neck matches her plush.

Lefty the Donkey

- ➤ Style: 4086
- ➤ Birthday: 7-4-96
- ➤ Released: 6-15-96
- ➤ Retired: 1-1-97
- ➤ Hangtag: 4

Lefty and Righty the elephant are the only Beanies that share both a birthday and a poem. Ty trotted out the same body style as Derby the horse for this steel-blue donkey, but his mane and tail are black instead of brown. He also has black hooves, nose, and inner ears.

Get the Scoop

As the Democratic candidate for the 1996 Presidential election, Lefty was retired before the inauguration.

Snort the Bull

- ➤ Style: 4002
- ➤ Birthday: 5-15-95
- ➤ Released: 1-1-97
- ➤ Retired: 9-15-98
- ➤ Hangtag: 4-5

When Tabasco the bull was benched, Snort came to play center court. The two are almost identical; the only difference is that Snort has cream-colored hooves.

Get the Scoop

Some Snorts were shipped with Tabasco's tag, and some Canadian Snorts have "Snort" as the name on the tag, but Tabasco's name in the poem.

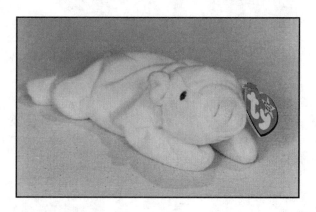

Squealer the Pig

- ➤ Style: 4005
- ➤ Birthday: 4-23-93
- ➤ Released: 1-8-94
- ➤ Retired: 5-1-98
- ➤ Hangtag: 1-5

Squealer's little folded ears and pink knotted tail are endearing, though I have to admit a personal attachment to this Original Nine Beanie as he was one of the first I got.

Get the Scoop

Squealer, like his fellow retiree Zip, seemed to disappear from store shelves for several months prior to his retirement. As a result, he's generally a little more expensive than the rest of his retirement class.

Tabasco the Bull

➤ Style: 4002
➤ Birthday: 5-15-95
➤ Release: 6-3-95
➤ Retired: 1-1-97
➤ Hangtag: 3-4

It's the bull, NOT the sauce! But due to the name conflict, he had an untimely retirement—Snort was introduced with the same poem but the different name. You'll have to work hard to steer around the differences between these two: Tabasco's hooves are red, while Snort's are cream-colored like his nose, horns, and inner ears.

Get the Scoop

Thanks to his quick retirement, Tabasco's value shot through the barn roof—but now has finally stabilized.

Chapter 4

Birds of a Feather

In This Chapter

➤ Learn which bird Beanies make good holiday decorations

➤ Discover which Beanies make good gifts for patriotic collectibles, hunting themes, and bird lovers

➤ Tell the difference between some common counterfeit birds and the real thing!

If you've been flocking to the stores to stock up on bird Beanies, this chapter will tell you all you need to know! There is lots to learn about in the bird department: common counterfeits, some gorgeous plumage, and some connections to baseball promotions that are sure to continue. Read on for the details!

Baldy the Eagle

➤ Style: 4074
➤ Birthday: 2-17-96
➤ Released: 5-11-97
➤ Retired: 5-1-98
➤ Hangtag: 4-5

Baldy's black plush body makes a striking contrast to his white head and bright yellow beak and feet. Only released for a year, he flew into retirement recently enough that he's fairly easy to find if you want to start in on your collection of retired Beanies.

Get the Scoop

Because of his association with our national emblem, Baldy is a favorite among collectors of patriotic items as well as bird collectors and Beanie Baby fans.

Batty the Bat

- ➤ Style: 4035
- ➤ Birthday: 10-29-96
- ➤ Released: 10-1-97
- ➤ Retired:
- ➤ Hangtag: 4-5

Batty's plush is a difficult color to describe—it's a pinky-colored light brown, not a deep chocolate-colored brown like you might expect after watching all those old Boris Karloff movies. His felt ears and feet are the same color.

Get the Scoop

Unlike any other Beanie in the collection, Batty has Velcro on the edges of his wing tips so he can be stuck on you.

Caw the Crow

- ➤ Style: 4071
- ➤ Birthday: (none)
- ➤ Released: 6-3-95
- ➤ Retired: 6-15-96
- ➤ Hangtag: 3

Caw is a short, squat black plush with long tail and wings. His beak and feet are a bright orange plush. Though simple in name and design, he's very appealing in person, especially to bird lovers.

Get the Scoop

Caw wasn't on the market very long, which means people will pay more money to cage him in their collections.

Early the Robin

- ➤ Style: 4190
- ➤ Birthday: 3-20-97
- ➤ Released: 5-30-98
- ➤ Retired:
- ➤ Hangtag: 5

Early's plush is a deep brown tie-dye (the same as Pounce). Naturally, he sports a bright red plush chest like every good robin. He's one of the shortest Beanies and appeared with a whole flock of birds in the May 30, 1998 release.

Get the Scoop

If you're looking for a cheerful way to celebrate the spring, consider hosting a springtime brunch, and decorate your buffet table with Early.

Gracie the Swan

- ➤ Style: 4126
- ➤ Birthday: 6-17-96
- ➤ Released: 1-1-97
- ➤ Retired: 5-1-98
- ➤ Hangtag: 4-5

Gracie is another of those hard-to-keep-clean white Beanies, with bright orange feet and beak and black plastic eyes. Many felt she was too plain, but as a newly retired Beanie, she has gained popularity.

Get the Scoop

The Chicago Cubs used Gracie in a promotion to honor their first baseman, Mark Grace.

Hoot the Owl

- ➤ Style: 4073
- ➤ Birthday: 8-9-95
- ➤ Released: 1-7-96
- ➤ Retired: 10-1-97
- ➤ Hangtag: 3-4

Like many other bird Beanies, Hoot is another shortie. His rounded head, body, and the tops of his wings are dark-brown plush. His face, chest, and the undersides of his wings are a lighter brown (the same color as Derby), and he has a small orange felt beak. Some tags have an error where "quite" is spelled "qutie."

Get the Scoop

For a long time, buyers did not exactly flock to the stores to stock up on this poor little bird, whom many consider to be a less-than-exciting example of the Beanie Baby art. As a retiree, he may gain slowly in value.

Jabber the Parrot

- ➤ Style: 4197
- ➤ Birthday: 10-10-97
- ➤ Released: 5-30-98
- ➤ Retired:
- ➤ Hangtag: 5

Jabber is one of the most colorful Beanies of all, similar in style to his predecessors Caw and Kiwi. A bright red Beanie, the top of his head is bright blue, while the top of his beak, the undersides of his wings, and his feet are yellow. The wings closest to the body are green, changing to blue plush halfway down, and his eyes are yellow surrounded by black-and-white striped plush.

Get the Scoop

Jabber was one of a group of 14 new babies introduced May 30, 1998.

Jake the Mallard Duck

- ➤ Style: 4199
- ➤ Birthday: 4-16-97
- ➤ Released: 5-30-98
- ➤ Retired:
- ➤ Hangtag: 5

Jake is a beautiful rendition of the real thing: His head is a deep teal green (deeper than teal Teddy), and he has a white neck band, light gray sides and back, and dark gray on his wing tops. The teal material is repeated on the top of his tail. His chest matches the tie-dyed brown material worn by Pounce and Early, and his beak is gold felt, stitched in black around the edge with embroidered nostrils. His feet are the same material as his beak.

Get the Scoop

Jake is popular not just with Beanie fans, but with those who enjoy decorating their dens in a hunting motif.

Kiwi the Toucan

- ➤ Style: 4070
- ➤ Birthday: 9-16-95
- ➤ Released: 6-3-95
- ➤ Retired: 1-1-97
- ➤ Hangtag: 3-4

Bright Kiwi looks a lot like Caw in the body department:
The plush on the top of his head, back, wings, and tail is
black, but his chest and the bottom of his wings are bright
red. The underside of his head and neck is bright yellow,
and the blue used on his long beak is the same as the
royal blue used in the rare version of Peanut.

On the Sly

Accept no substitutes! The counterfeit
Kiwi's beak is a lighter blue and much
shorter than the legitimate version.

Kuku the Cockatoo

- ➤ Style: 4192
- ➤ Birthday: 1-5-97
- ➤ Released: 5-30-98
- ➤ Retired:
- ➤ Hangtag: 5

Besides his bright white plush body and wings and gray beak and feet, it's hard to miss Kuku's shocking crown of bright pink fluff on the top of his head.

Get the Scoop

Looking a bit like a punk rock star without the nose ring, Kuku is one of six Beanie birds released at the end of May 1998.

Pinky the Flamingo

- ➤ Style: 4072
- ➤ Birthday: 2-13-95
- ➤ Released: 6-3-95
- ➤ Retired:
- ➤ Hangtag: 3-5

Pinky truly fits her name: Her body plush is bright pink, a color not found on any other Beanie. Her long, dangling light pink legs allow her to be draped over almost anything, and her bright orange beak is the same color as Goldie. Pinky's Teenie Beanie counterpart is the most rare and valuable Teenie from the 1997 set.

On the Sly

The "red Pinky" rumored as a new Ty release turned out to be nothing more than another counterfeit.

Puffer the Puffin

- ➤ Style: 4181
- ➤ Birthday: 11-3-97
- ➤ Released: 12-31-97
- ➤ Retired: 9-18-98
- ➤ Hangtag: 5

Puffer's black back and white chest look terrific next to her red feet and beak banded with yellow and red. The sides of her face are white plush with a small triangle of black material surrounding her eyes.

Get the Scoop

After the May 1998 retirement, Puffer was left with only two other birds in the current category until the May 1998 new releases that brought in six new birds. Retired only nine months after his release, look for his value to rise a bit more than the average Beanie.

Quackers the Duck

- ➤ Style: 4024
- ➤ Birthday: (none) (wingless)
- ➤ Birthday: 4-19-94 (winged)
- ➤ Released: 6-25-94 (wingless)
- ➤ Released: 1-7-95 (winged)
- ➤ Retired: 1-7-95 (wingless)
- ➤ Retired: 5-1-98 (winged)
- ➤ Hangtag: 1-2 (wingless)
- ➤ Hangtag: 2-5 (winged)

The awkward-looking original version of Quackers is quite rare. Without his wings and with generally less "beans" than the later winged version, Quackers had a hard time keeping his balance. Both versions are covered in bright yellow plush, with stuffed orange beaks, orange feet, and embroidered eyebrows.

Get the Scoop

Either version of Quackers (winged or plucked) may have old swing tags that made his name singular (Quacker).

Radar the Bat

- ➤ Style: 4091
- ➤ Birthday: 10-30-95
- ➤ Released: 9-1-95
- ➤ Retired: 5-11-97
- ➤ Hangtag: 3-4

The only break from Radar's all-black plush and felt feet and "fingertips" is the white plush inside his ears and two little beady red eyes. Though finding Radar isn't difficult, finding one in mint condition that hasn't been played with into oblivion is a little more challenging!

Get the Scoop

If you're looking for a good Halloween decoration, search no farther! This cute little black bat will look smashing as part of your holiday decorations.

Scoop the Pelican

➤ Style: 4107
➤ Birthday: 7-1-96
➤ Released: 6-15-96
➤ Retired:
➤ Hangtag: 4-5

Dressed in the same steel-blue plush as Echo and Crunch, Scoop's distinguishing feature is a huge stuffed bill of bright orange plush. Too bad for Scoop it's not stuffed with fish! Scoop's feet are made from the same bright orange plush.

Get the Scoop

Scoop gained popularity when he was included in the 1998 Teenie Beanie set.

Stretch the Ostrich

➤ Style: 4182
➤ Birthday: 9-21-97
➤ Released: 12-31-97
➤ Retired:
➤ Hangtag: 5

Stretch was the hardest to find of the new year's releases for quite a while. Resembling her cousin Pinky the flamingo, Stretch shares Pinky's long dangling legs, but in tan rather than pink. Her long slender neck is the same color. Her body is brown, but her wing tips are white. Most notable is the fluffy white necklace of fur she wears day and night.

Get the Scoop

A commemorative Stretch was given away as a memento at the St. Louis Cardinals game on May 22, 1998.

Wise the Owl

- ➤ Style: 4194
- ➤ Birthday: 5-31-97
- ➤ Released: 5-30-98
- ➤ Retired:
- ➤ Hangtag: 5

What a hoot! Don't expect this Beanie to be flapping around for long. The second of what Ty seems to intend as "annual Beanies" sells out quickly in anticipation of a year-end retirement. Similarly styled to Hoot, Wise is taller even without the black mortarboard and bright orange tassel proclaiming his graduation.

Get the Scoop

Wait to see if you can find Wise in a store before paying secondary prices for him.

The original nine: Chocolate, Squealer, Cubbie, Patti, Flash, Splash, Pinchers, Legs, and Spot.

Mid-1994 releases: Slither, Daisy, Speedy, Blackie, Chilly, Web, Ally, Lucky, Humphrey, tan Inky (no mouth), Mystic, Quackers (wingless), orange Digger, gray Happy, Bones, Goldie, Teal (old face), Magenta (old face), Violet (old face), Brown (old face), and Jade (old face).

Early 1995 releases: light blue Peanut, black and blue Lizzy, Inch, Ringo, Tusk, Bucky, Flip, Tank, Radar, Derby, Grunt, Mystic, Manny, Bumble, Weenie, Patti, Twigs, Coral, Ears, Seaweed, Garcia, Spooky, white-paw Nip, white-paw Zip, Hoot, and Pinky.

Mid-1995 releases: (darkish) magenta Patti, Nana/Bongo, tan Inky with mouth, Valentino/all-gold Nip, white-face Nip, white-face Zip, all-black Zip, Quackers with wings, Jade (new face), Violet (new face), Cranberry (new face), Brown (new face), Teal (new face), Magenta (new face), and Spooky.

Early 1996 releases: Flutter, Sting, Ziggy, Stinky, red Digger, pink Inky, tie-dye Lizzy, Bubbles, Steg, Waddle, Kiwi, Caw, fine-mane Derby, royal blue Peanut, dark Stripes, lilac Happy, Rex, Tabasco, Bronty, Bessie, Bongo, Magic, and Velvet.

Mid-1996 releases: Rover, Wrinkles, Sparky, Freckles, Righty, Lefty, Scottie, Spike, Scoop, Libearty, Curly, Congo, and brown-bellied Sly.

January 1997 releases: Snort, Doby, Snip, Mel, Crunch, Bernie, Fleece, Hippity, Pouch, Gracie, Hoppity, Nuts, Floppity, and Maple.

May 1997 releases: (dark) Claude, Chip, Dotty, Roary, Nanook, Tuffy, Blizzard, Pugsly, Baldy, Jolly, Echo, Waves, Doodle, and Peace.

October 1997 releases: Spinner, Batty, Gobbles, Snowball, and 1997 Teddy.

January 1998 releases: Prance, Spunky, Pounce, Bruno, Rainbow-Iggy, Iggy-Rainbow, Hissy, Puffer, Stretch, and Smoochy.

Mid-1998 releases: Stinger, Gigi, Fetch, Early, Whisper, Tracker, Ants, Jabber, Jake, Rocket, Wise, Glory, Fortune, and Kuku.

McDonald's Teenie Beanie Babies, the first set.

McDonald's Teenie Beanie Babies, the second set.

Peanuts with peanuts.

I ♥ Beanies: Britannia the Engineer, Snip the Clown, Fortune ready for bed, Brown Moose (old face), Glory the spaceman, Blackie the ladybug, Princess in her jogging suit, Violet Bee (new face), Teal Clown (old face), and Valentino out of the shower.

Tie-dye Claude, Flutter, Sting, Iggy-Rainbow, Coral, tie-dye Lizzy, Steg, Rex, Peace, Bronty, Garcia, and Doodle.

Pumpkin Curly.

Jabber, Kuku, Caw, Early, Rocket, Kiwi, and Baldy.

Patriotic Righty, Lefty, Britannia, Libearty, Glory, and Maple.

Floppity, Hippity, and Hoppity.

Noah's Ark: Scottie, Patti, Pugsly, Humphrey, Chilly, Prance, Strut, Chops, Bongo, Ally, Quackers, Hissy, Legs, Happy, Peanut, Daisy, Derby, Squealer, Bones, and Fleece.

The wedding: Valentino, Cranberry (new face), Teal (new face), Daisy, and Snort.

Garcia, Peace, and Woodstock tickets.

The colored Teddys.

Inky: tan–no mouth, pink, and tan with mouth.

Princess and Erin.

In the limo: Whisper, Stinger, Tracker, Fetch, Kuku, Glory, Ants, Fortune, Gigi, Jake, Early, Jabber, Wise, and Rocket.

Spike the green iguana shares carrots with Iggy and Rainbow.

Chocolate, Chip, cookies, and milk.

Valentino comes bearing gifts.

White- and brown-belly Sly.

Patti: raspberry, magenta, and fuchsia.

Chapter 5

Bow-Wowing the Critics

In This Chapter

➤ Learn why Sparky was transformed into Dotty

➤ Discover why Fetch the Golden Retriever is so plain

➤ Collar all the details on which Beanie pups are the most popular, and why

It's a dog's life, and nobody knows that better than the Ty company, which seems to delight in releasing packs of hounds in a variety of irresistible shapes, sizes, and designs. In this chapter you'll read about some of the extraordinarily well-done details of the Beanie dogs, such as the sewn-in wrinkles on Pugsly and Wrinkles, the tiny red bows on Gigi the Poodle, and those soulful sad eyes of Tracker the Basset.

Whether you're a dog lover who would like to buy a few Beanies, or a Beanie fanatic who's interested in some excellent designs, you'll find out all you need to know in this chapter.

Bernie the St. Bernard

➤ Style: 4109
➤ Birthday: 10-3-96
➤ Released: 1-1-97
➤ Retired: 9-22-98
➤ Hangtag: 4-5

If you love St. Bernards but hate the slobber, this one's for you! Bernie is a lay-down St. Bernard with tan, black, and cream plush. He sports a cream streak along the top of his head and around his muzzle, with black patches of plush around his eyes (but no whiskey under his chin).

Get the Scoop

This St. Bernard was fairly common, so you shouldn't have much trouble rescuing one at your neighborhood Beanie dealer, even though he's retired.

Bones the Dog

- ➤ Style: 4001
- ➤ Birthday: 1-18-94
- ➤ Released: 6-25-94
- ➤ Retired: 5-1-98
- ➤ Hangtag: 1-5

Bones has that hang-dog, hound-dog look, with a tan body and long brown ears and tail. His wide black nose and eyebrows give him a "surprised" look, and he's one of the earliest Beanies you can still find on the shelves.

Get the Scoop

Bones was one of the Teenie Beanie Babies released in May 1998 in the second, overwhelmingly popular McDonald's promotion.

Bruno the Terrier

- ➤ Style: 4183
- ➤ Birthday: 9-9-97
- ➤ Released: 12-31-97
- ➤ Retired: 9-18-98
- ➤ Hangtag: 5

Most likely modeled after a bull terrier, Bruno was a January 1998 release with dark brown back and ears, and white belly, paws, nose, and tail tip. Pictures of him don't do him justice: In person, he's irresistible.

Get the Scoop

Bruno's retirement in September, 1998, came as a surprise to collectors. As a "short-timer" in the Beanie kennel, his value will probably increase more than some of the Beanies retired in the same time frame.

Doby the Doberman

- ➤ Style: 4110
- ➤ Birthday: 10-9-96
- ➤ Released: 1-1-97
- ➤ Retired:
- ➤ Hangtag: 4-5

Like the look of a Doberman but worry about all those teeth? Park this little fellow by your door and relax! Little black Doby has brown paws, underbelly, under ears, and nose, with two brown eyebrows giving him a perpetual look of surprise. His ears are long, just the way real Dobermans are born.

Get the Scoop

Doby had the distinction of being number one in the second series of McDonald's Teenie Beanie Babies.

Dotty the Dalmatian

- ➤ Style: 4100
- ➤ Birthday: 10-17-96
- ➤ Released: 5-11-97
- ➤ Retired:
- ➤ Hangtag: 4-5

Dotty replaced Sparky quicker than a dog can bury a pork chop, as a result of yet another name conflict. If you're looking for the difference between Dotty and Sparky, check out the ears and tail: Dotty's are black, while Sparky's are white-spotted.

Get the Scoop

Alert Beanie collectors were tipped off to Dotty's impending birth when "Dotty" tush tags started cropping up on the last of the Sparkys.

Fetch the Golden Retriever

- ➤ Style: 4189
- ➤ Birthday: 2-4-97
- ➤ Released: 5-30-98
- ➤ Retired:
- ➤ Hangtag: 5

Needless to say, this little pup is made of golden plush. The plain-faced Fetch dismayed owners of the breed, but for those of you who want to split doghairs: Golden Retriever puppies don't develop their "feathers" until later in life, so this little guy is anatomically correct.

Get the Scoop

As the mascot of one of the most popular of all dog breeds, many collectors suspect that Fetch will soon become hard to find.

Gigi the Poodle

➤ Style: 4191
➤ Birthday: 4-7-98
➤ Released: 5-30-98
➤ Retired:
➤ Hangtag: 5

Gigi is the first Beanie to be made of both smooth and
napped plush as a nod to the typical tufted hairdo you'll
find on real Poodles. Similar in body shape to retired Scottie, Gigi is beautifully made, with all the elegant details
you'd expect in a Parisian pooch: black fur, black nose,
and tiny twin red ribbons decorating her ears.

Get the Scoop

Poodles are said to be among the very
most intelligent of all dog breeds.
Gigi's lively little face should be a very
popular seller among Poodle lovers and Beanie
collectors alike.

Nanook the Husky

- ➤ Style: 4104
- ➤ Birthday: 11-21-96
- ➤ Released: 5-11-97
- ➤ Retired:
- ➤ Hangtag: 4-5

If you've got a yen for a Beanie with a big, round head, pudgy body, and sweet blue eyes, you'll want to rub noses with Nanook the husky dog. It's been a real sled race among collectors, who began searching for this pooch once he became hard to find in 1997. His back, head, and the backs of his ears are dark gray plush; while his face, inner ears, belly, and paws are white.

Get the Scoop
If you've spent long months fruitlessly mushing down the trails looking for Nanook, you'll be pleased to know collectors report that he is becoming easier to find.

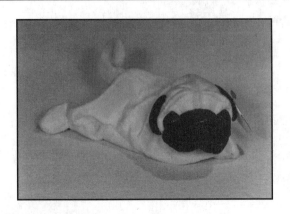

Pugsly the Pug Dog

- ➤ Style: 4106
- ➤ Birthday: 5-2-96
- ➤ Released: 5-11-97
- ➤ Retired:
- ➤ Hangtag: 4-5

Get the Scoop

Pugsly was one of four dogs introduced on Mother's Day 1997.

Little Pugsly is created from beige plush with black inner ears and snout to resemble the real thing. Like all self-respecting Pugs, Pugsly has a wrinkly forehead, thanks to rows of wrinkles stitched into his forehead that give him a worried frown. If you're pugnacious, you'll be able to find this current release fairly easily in stores.

Rover the Dog

- ➤ Style: 4101
- ➤ Birthday: 5-30-96
- ➤ Released: 6-15-96
- ➤ Retired: 5-1-98
- ➤ Hangtag: 4-5

With his bright, lobster-colored plush and long, round face, Rover closely resembles Clifford the Big Red Dog, hero of a series of children's books. Rover has long ears and an oval black plastic nose like those used on many of the new-faced bears. He's one of the more difficult-to-find Beanies from the May 1998 retirements, in part because he was snatched up so eagerly by preschoolers already familiar with Clifford.

Get the Scoop

If you've got preschoolers on your gift list, think about putting a leash around Rover, a real favorite among this age group because of his similarity to Clifford.

Scottie the Scottish Terrier

➤ Style: 4102
➤ Birthday: 6-15-96
➤ Released: 6-15-96
➤ Retired: 5-1-98
➤ Hangtag: 4-5

You don't need to be the Laird of Loch Lomond to hanker after this little Scottie, one of the few Beanies sharing nappy plush. Jet black with a body style similar to Gigi the Poodle, some collectors growl that Scottie's face is too dark to stand out properly.

Get the Scoop

Don't be surprised if your Scottie has a birthday of June 6 instead of June 15! Both dates exist on the tags, but neither is considered more valuable than the other.

Sparky the Dalmatian

- ➤ Style: 4100
- ➤ Birthday: 2-27-96
- ➤ Released: 6-15-96
- ➤ Retired: 5-11-97
- ➤ Hangtag: 4

Some days, it must seem like a dog's life at the Ty company, where trademark infringements seem to pop up faster than toadstools after a spring rain. Case in point: Sparky, who produced yet another renaming when the National Fire Protection Association folks pointed out they had first dibs on the "Sparky the Fire Dog." As a result, his name and image were subsequently re-released as Dotty. The difference between the two? Sparky's white-spotted ears and tail (Dotty's are black).

Get the Scoop

Alert collectors noted that the last Sparkys to come rolling off the assembly line were equipped with "Dotty" tush tags.

Spot the Dog

- ➤ Style: 4000
- ➤ Birthday: (none) (no spot)
- ➤ Birthday: 1-3-93 (spot)
- ➤ Released: 1-8-94 (no spot)
- ➤ Released: 4-13-94 (spot)
- ➤ Retired: 4-13-94 (no spot)
- ➤ Retired: 10-1-97 (spot)
- ➤ Hangtag: 1 (no spot)
- ➤ Hangtag: 1-4 (spot)

No matter how hard you try, you won't be able to spot the spot on the original Spot. This little Beanie was first issued with a partly black face, black ears, and tail—but strangely enough, no spot on the back. Hence, his nicknames: "Spotless Spot" or "Spot without a Spot." The spotless version didn't last long and was replaced with the more common spotted variety, with a half-circle on the left half of his back.

On the Sly

There have been reports of false spotless Spots—beware! The real spot-free pooch is extremely rare and pricey. If you don't see spots when you're shopping for Spot, it pays to put on your specs to make sure you've got the real thing.

Spunky the Cocker Spaniel

➤ Style: 4184
➤ Birthday: 1-14-97
➤ Released: 12-31-97
➤ Retired:
➤ Hangtag: 5

Spunky quickly became one of the most popular Beanies from the December 31, 1997 releases. Handsome in tan plush, he's got that typical big domed head so characteristic of cockers. If you're lucky, you'll be able to sniff out a Spunky to add to your collection!

Get the Scoop

Like the true Cocker Spaniels who inspired him, Spunky's ears are covered with long, soft curls—the only Beanie Baby with such curly plush.

Tracker the Basset Hound

➤ Style: 4198
➤ Birthday: 6-5-97
➤ Released: 5-30-98
➤ Retired:
➤ Hangtag: 5

If you've got a nose for a good buy, sniff your way to the nearest shop with the most recently released Beanie pup— the sad-eyed Tracker. It may take some time before this brown-and-white hound shows up as a regular on store shelves.

Get the Scoop

No doubt those doleful eyes (unique to Tracker) and long plush ears will make him one of the more popular dogs in the Beanie kennel.

Tuffy the Terrier

- ➤ Style: 4108
- ➤ Birthday: 10-12-96
- ➤ Released: 5-11-97
- ➤ Retired:
- ➤ Hangtag: 4-5

Tuffy is a nappy (not a yappy) terrier. Similar in body style to Gigi and Scottie, Tuffy is the only two-tone nappy Beanie. Ty uses the same tan plush on Tuffy and Curly the bear, but the brown nappy plush on Tuffy's back is unique to him.

Get the Scoop

What's the doggone quickest way to find out whether you have an older or a newer Tuffy? Check out his name on the tag. Early releases spelled his name in capital letters.

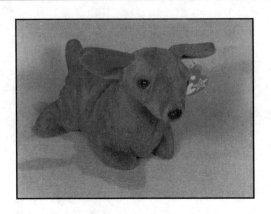

Weenie the Dachshund

➤ Style: 4013
➤ Birthday: 7-20-95
➤ Released: 1-7-96
➤ Retired: 5-1-98
➤ Hangtag: 3-5

Quite a hot dog before his retirement (Weenie was easy to find in just about every retail store!), Weenie is now one of the harder-to-find members of the May 1998 retirement pack. His plush may be plain bone-brown, but his long body and wide-spread ears make him a popular pooch.

Get the Scoop

Weenie's plush comes in two kinds of brown: shiny and less shiny. Make no bones about it, though—either coat is worth about the same.

Wrinkles the Bulldog

- ➤ Style: 4103
- ➤ Birthday: 5-1-96
- ➤ Released: 6-15-96
- ➤ Retired: 9-22-98
- ➤ Hangtag: 4-5

This gold and white plush pup lives up to his name, with more wrinkles than a day-old leisure suit. His sewn-in wrinkles on back and face guarantee that authentic worried look of the bulldog, and resemble Pugsly, the other wrinkled Beanie.

Get the Scoop

The recently retired Wrinkles has two larger cousins in the plush line (named Winston and Churchill) as well as a Pillow Pal cousin. Collect all four for a great display!

Chapter 6

Creepy-Crawlers

In This Chapter

➤ Learn the different permutations of Lucky the ladybug and all her spots

➤ Uncover the manufacturing mix-up between Iggy and Rainbow

➤ Find lots of decorating ideas with these Beanie Babies

If it's creepy and crawly, lizardy or spidery, you'll likely find it in this chapter. Yet even these stuffed critters, despite their names, are more cuties than creepies. We've taken quite a few liberties with the Beanies we've included here—after all, alligators are not really anywhere near the same genus as a bumblebee or a butterfly. But if you look at one of these animals and shiver, you'll likely find its Beanie counterpart within this chapter!

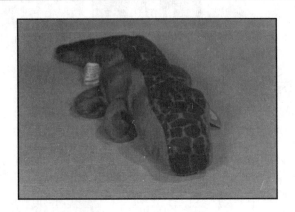

Ally the Alligator

➤ Style: 4032
➤ Birthday: 3-14-94
➤ Released: 6-25-94
➤ Retired: 10-1-97
➤ Hangtag: 1-4

If you're a University of Florida grad, you've probably already wrestled this little alligator from the gift shop out to the parking lot. The rest of you are probably lining up for Ally not because he's a mascot, but just because he's so cute! About a foot long with avocado-green sides and stomach, he's got a strip of brown spots on avocado-green along his back.

Get the Scoop

How can you tell whether an alligator is a boy or a girl? By the poem! (At least you can if it's a Ty Beanie Baby...) Even though Ally often gets referred to as a "she" because of his name, the poem definitely indicates he's all boy.

Bumble the Bee

➤ Style: 4045
➤ Birthday: (none)
➤ Released: 6-3-95
➤ Retired: 6-15-96
➤ Hangtag: 3-4

Feeling down in the dumps? Buying this little fellow can take the sting out of a bad day! Bumble is small, even as Beanies go—he can fit right into the palm of your hand. Looking typically bee-like with a yellow-and-black striped back, he also has a black head, wings, and underbelly.

Get the Scoop

Bumble is the one exception to the "older tags are more valuable" rule—his fourth-generation version is more rare than the one before it.

Flutter the Butterfly

➤ Style: 4043
➤ Birthday: (none)
➤ Released: 6-3-95
➤ Retired: 6-15-96
➤ Hangtag: 3

If you really want to butter up a collecting friend, try giving Flutter as a gift! Usually found in bright rainbow tie-dye, Flutter can also appear in more subtle tones. Only the lower rounded part of her wings are heavily stuffed with "beans"; both her body and the upper part of her wings contain little stuffing. Her black plush body is matched by long black antennae waving at the top of her head.

On the Sly

Look closely and you'll see that Flutter has knotted eyes rather than the hard plastic ones found on most other Beanies. One variation of a counterfeit Flutter has appeared with hard plastic eyes, so if you see these—fly away and don't buy!

Hissy the Snake

➤ Style: 4185
➤ Birthday: 4-4-97
➤ Released: 12-31-98
➤ Retired:
➤ Hangtag: 5

If you're the type who likes to fiddle with something in your hands, then Hissy is the Beanie for you. One of Ty's most innovative Beanie designs, Hissy's natural stretchy coil just begs to be played with. The top of Hissy's plush is blue tie-dyed like Bronty and Sting, but his underside is bright yellow like Quackers the duck. A red ribbon tongue completes his reptilian charm.

Get the Scoop

Because of the unique coiled design of this Beanie, you can get some really nifty display effects by wrapping him around another object. Don't just line 'em all up—be creative! Coil, drape, hang, or weave this beautiful Beanie to add zest to your collection.

Iggy the Iguana

➤ Style: 4038
➤ Birthday: 8-12-97
➤ Released: 12-31-97 (bright tie-dye without a tongue)
➤ Released: about mid-May, 1998 (bright tie-dye with a tongue)
➤ Released: about mid-August, 1998 (blue tie-dye without a tongue)
➤ Retired: about mid-May, 1998 (bright tie-dye without a tongue)
➤ Retired: about mid-August, 1998 (bright tie-dye with a tongue)
➤ Retired: (blue tie-dye without a tongue)
➤ Hangtag: 5

It's doubtful that Bette Davis had Iggy in mind when she agreed to star in Tennessee Williams' "Night of the Iguana"—but although he's never been onstage, this version is pretty darn cute! Iggy has yellow plastic eyes and a cheek-to-cheek yellow mouth that aren't found on any other Beanie.

On the Sly

If you're the type who gets confused as to who's on first, then don't try to decipher the saga of Iggy the iguana and Rainbow the chameleon! For months collectors thought it was their tags that were reversed, but as it turns out, it really was their plush coats. Just remember that no matter what his coat color, whether it be bright tie-dye like Peace, Garcia, or Coral, or blue tie-dye like Bronty and Sting, you're looking at Iggy the iguana. If you're looking at a Beanie reptile with a flap of plush behind his head (and no felt spikes along his back), you've got Iggy's pal Rainbow in your hands, even if he's blue. The second variation of Iggy (a bright tie-dyed version) has a soft pink tongue, but when the plush was corrected, the tongue moved, too, leaving poor Iggy tongue-tied.

Inch the Worm

➤ Style: 4044
➤ Birthday: 9-3-95
➤ Released: 6-3-95 (felt)
➤ Released: 10-15-96 (yarn)
➤ Retired: 10-15-96 (felt)
➤ Retired: 5-1-98 (yarn)
➤ Hangtag: 3-4 (felt)
➤ Hangtag: 4-5 (yarn)

He's long, he's wiggly, and he's stiff enough to stand up on end—he's Inch, the multicolored Beanie who's wormed his way into many collectors' hearts! Unlike many other Beanies, he's not a tie-dye—his colors are divided neatly into sections, sort of like a patchwork quilt laid end-to-end. His head starts off in yellow, followed by sections of bright orange, lime green, royal blue, and bright orchid.

Get the Scoop

If you've packed your Inch up into a Ziploc bag to put away as an investment, inch on over and check out his antennae. Originally released with felt antennae, these gave way to yarn in late 1996; the felt feelers are worth more than the yarn variety. Which have you got?

Lizzy the Lizard

- ➤ Style: 4033
- ➤ Birthday: (none) (tie-dyed)
- ➤ Birthday: 5-11-95 (blue)
- ➤ Released: 6-3-95 (tie-dyed)
- ➤ Released: 1-7-96 (blue)
- ➤ Retired: 1-7-96 (tie-dyed)
- ➤ Retired: 12-31-97 (blue)
- ➤ Hangtag: 3 (tie-dyed)
- ➤ Hangtag: 3-4 (blue)

Unbeknownst to many collectors, the original-release Lizzy was resplendent in an earth-toned tie-dye plush rather than the black-on-blue spotted plush she now wears. As with all tie-dyed Beanies, each of these Lizzies is unique and her value may depend on her coloring as well as her condition. The black-on-blue version has orange-on-yellow plush on her belly.

On the Sly

Lizzy's felt tongue seems to end up taking most of the abuse, so if you're a collector who wants to preserve the condition of your Beanies, you might take particular care of this lizard part.

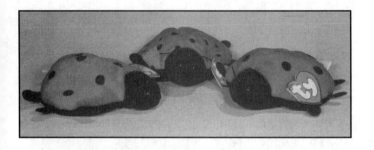

Lucky the Ladybug

- ➤ Style: 4040
- ➤ Birthday: (none) (7 spot)
- ➤ Birthday: 5-1-95 (21 spot)
- ➤ Birthday: 5-1-95 (11 spot)
- ➤ Released: 6-25-94 (7 spot)
- ➤ Released: circa 2-25-96 (21 spot)
- ➤ Released: circa 6-15-96 (11 spot)
- ➤ Retired: circa 2-27-96 (7 spot)
- ➤ Retired: circa 6-15-96 (21 spot)
- ➤ Retired: 5-1-98 (11 spot)
- ➤ Hangtag: 1-3 (7 spot)
- ➤ Hangtag: 4 (21 spot)
- ➤ Hangtag: 4-5 (11 spot)

A leopard may not be able to change his spots, but that hasn't stopped Lucky the ladybug: Proving that a lady can always change her mind, she's swapped her spots at least five times. Her original design included 7 spots of felt glued onto her red plush back—but when those spots started falling off, it was back to the drawing board for Ty. Voilá! Her plush changed to preprinted spots—21 of them. However, the 21-spot version turned out to be short-lived; while a more common recent variation has about 11 printed spots, she may appear with as few as 8 and as many as 14. In addition to her spots, she also has a black head, black string antennae, black belly, and six felt legs.

Get the Scoop

When she first appeared, Lucky the 21-spotted ladybug wasn't exactly flying off the shelves—but today those few who bought her are glad they did!

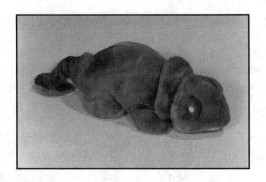

Rainbow the Chameleon

- ➤ Style: 4037
- ➤ Birthday: 10-14-97
- ➤ Released: 12-31-97 (blue tie-dyed without a tongue)
- ➤ Released: about mid-August, 1998 (bright tie-dye with a tongue)
- ➤ Retired: about mid-August, 1998 (blue tie-dyed without a tongue)
- ➤ Retired: (bright tie-dye with a tongue)
- ➤ Hangtag: 5

It's true that chameleons change their color at the drop of a hat, so you shouldn't be surprised if the creature you've been calling Rainbow because of his bright tie-dyed plush really turned out to be Iggy the iguana sporting the wrong coat! Most people thought their tags were mixed up, but those collectors really in the know about all things reptilian figured out that it was the chameleons that wore that little hood behind their heads and iguanas had spikes. They called it right, and the old blue tie-dyed Rainbow hit the streets while the new and improved bright tie-dyed Rainbow came in from the cold. And if that wasn't enough to keep your tongue wagging, the pink tongue that the second version of Iggy had has migrated to the new and improved Rainbow!

It makes you wonder if it should be on the blue Iggy, though.

Get the Scoop

Check out that little pink velveteen tongue flapping in the front of the brightly tie-dyed Rainbow since around mid-August. Beginning with mid-year shipments, that same tongue had been found on Iggy the iguana, not Rainbow! All bets are off as to whether it stays on the bright tie-dyed chameleon or wags its way back to the now-blue Iggy.

Slither the Snake

- ➤ Style: 4031
- ➤ Birthday: (none)
- ➤ Released: 6-25-94
- ➤ Retired: 6-15-95
- ➤ Hangtag: 1-3

This two-foot-long reptile's back is covered in the spotted brown-on-green plush found on both Ally and Speedy. He's a real yellow-belly—bright yellow, the same plush as Quackers. He's also quite rare and very pricey—so if you're cold-blooded enough to stand the sticker shock, slither on over and check him out!

On the Sly

Slither's long red felt tongue is split down the middle and isn't as sturdy as the rest of him, so take care you don't pull it out by the roots when you're playing with him!

Smoochy the Frog

➤ Style: 4039
➤ Birthday: 10-1-97
➤ Released: 12-31-97
➤ Retired:
➤ Hangtag: 5

Perhaps this design was Ty's way of contrasting Smoochy with the plain styling of Legs the frog, but this amphibian got all the looks in the family. He's bright and far more intricate, with lime-green plush covering his back and neon yellow on all four feet and the front of his eyes. If you have to kiss a lot of frogs before you find your prince, here's hoping they all are as irresistible as Smoochy!

Get the Scoop

Smoochy's lips are red and created out of several different materials, none of which has earned a higher value than another at this point. So choose the one you like and wait and see!

Spinner the Spider

- ➤ Style: 4026
- ➤ Birthday: 10-28-96
- ➤ Released: 10-1-97
- ➤ Retired: 9-19-98
- ➤ Hangtag: 4-5

Most collectors agree that Spinner is pretty creepy—creepy enough that some were released with tush tags emblazoned with the name "Creepy." Nobody's sure if the Creepy tags are a harbinger of Beanies-to-be or a last-minute renaming of Spinner. Spinner's back is black-on-dark gold stripes, and he's also inherited Radar's red eyes. Retired after only one year as a current, Spinner spent only one Halloween scaring collectors away. They'll be running to entangle him now!

Get the Scoop

Planning a Halloween party and just can't find the right decorating touch? Don't look any further than the evil-looking Spinner, who's been known to give little kids nightmares. However, you may have to search quite a few webs before you land this little retired fellow: He's rare and getting rarer every minute.

Stinger the Scorpion

- ➤ Style: 4193
- ➤ Birthday: 9-29-97
- ➤ Released: 5-30-98
- ➤ Retired:
- ➤ Hangtag: 5

If astrology's your game, then all you Scorpios out there will be clamoring for this little stuffed scorpion, the sign of the eighth house of the zodiac. While a tad creepy-looking, his plush color is unique among Beanies: It's a deep taupe color. He's a Beanie who's not very photo-genic; he's much cuter in person.

On the Sly

Like his multi-legged friend Inky, Stinger sometimes gets a leg added or subtracted in his manufacture, so count them closely.

Web the Spider

- ➤ Style: 4041
- ➤ Birthday: (none)
- ➤ Released: 6-25-94
- ➤ Retired: 1-7-96
- ➤ Hangtag: 1-3

From the top, Web looks plain as can be, but flip this fellow over and you'll get a surprise: No, not an hourglass, but a belly of bright red plush. Unlike the later spider (Spinner), Web's eyes are black, not red, although red would be a perfect complement to his stomach.

Get the Scoop

If you've managed to trap this Beanie Baby, you'll want to spin a web around him quick, because he's hard to find and getting harder by the minute. Expect his value to rise, especially around Halloween!

Unbearably Cute

Even if you've bearly begun collecting Beanies, you'll probably be attracted to these colorful ursines—a whole wide range of adorable bears in a variety of colors. In fact, collectors of all sorts of stuffed bears enjoy collecting the bear group of Beanies, which are available in a huge range of colors (black, brown, cranberry, jade, magenta, teal, violet, white, and tie-dyed). Most of the bears are retired: fifteen of them in all, including Chilly, Garcia, Libearty, Peking, all the colored Teddies, and all the old-faced Teddies.

While many people may think of Beanie bears as the traditional "teddy" type, we've also included other bear varieties, such as the black bear and the polar bear—so if it's a bear of any type you're hankering for, you're sure to find it here!

Blackie the Bear

- ➤ Style: 4011
- ➤ Birthday: 7-15-94
- ➤ Released: 6-25-94
- ➤ Retired: 9-15-98
- ➤ Hangtag: 1-5

If you like to keep your bears just lying around, then Blackie is the one for you; he's one of four "lay-down" style bears available in the Ty collection. And surprise, surprise! He's all black (except for his snout, which is brown). If you want to collect the rest of the entire set of lay-down bears, here's what you should be looking for: Chilly, Cubbie and Peking. All of the lay-down bears have been retired now, with Blackie being the last of the Quad Squad. Blackie and Cubbie should be pretty easy to find. Don't count on the same being true for Chilly and Peking!

Get the Scoop

The Chicago Bears used Blackie (he's a natural!) as a promotion for their Kids' Fan Club.

Britannia the Bear

➤ Style: 4601
➤ Birthday: 12-15-97
➤ Released: 12-31-97
➤ Retired:
➤ Hangtag: 5

It's a long hike from London to the United States, so if you manage to snag a Britannia—the bear that is exclusively distributed in the United Kingdom—you're either a world traveler or you've plopped down quite a few pounds sterling to cage this critter! Although some of these little ladies have found their way to the States, they are generally quite expensive—even though they haven't yet been retired. Britannia is a brown "new-faced" bear with a Union Jack embroidered on her chest and a deep red ribbon.

On the Sly

Check Britannia's tags closely for errors to make sure you're getting the real thing and not a counterfeit. These errors include a "scrunchy"-looking font on the yellow star on the front of her tag, misplacement of the ™ symbol, and a smaller print than normal on the tush tag.

Brownie the Bear

➤ Style: 4010
➤ Birthday: (none)
➤ Released: 1993
➤ Retired: (pre-Beanies)
➤ Hangtag: 1

Brownie the bear is a predecessor of Cubbie (one of the Original Nine Beanies)—in fact, you'll bearly notice the difference unless you take a close peek at the swing tag. In order to be Brownie and not Cubbie, he must have that tag with his name on it; otherwise, he's just considered to be a Cubbie and not worth as much money. Brownie is a "lay-down" style bear with brown plush and a tan snout.

Get the Scoop

Brownie is usually considered a "pre-Beanie," and so if you're armed and hunting for bears, you may not find him in every checklist.

Chilly the Polar Bear

➤ Style: 4012
➤ Birthday: (none)
➤ Released: 6-25-94
➤ Retired: 1-7-96
➤ Hangtag: 1-3

Chilly is probably the most popular of the four "lay-down" style bears—and like all highly desirable Beanies, one of the hardest to find. His all-white plush is difficult to keep clean. If you're a collector and you manage to trap one, put him in hibernation behind a plastic or glass case to keep him in mint condition. Dust and dirt are Chilly's enemy.

Get the Scoop

Two of the bear Beanies have collectible mistakes, so if you're in the mood for unique Beanie Babies, check out these two: Maple with the "Pride" tush tag (which makes him about three times more valuable than a "regular" Maple); and Libearty with a misspelled "beanine" tush tag (which is a common error).

Curly the Bear

- ➤ Style: 4052
- ➤ Birthday: 4-12-96
- ➤ Released: 6-15-96
- ➤ Retired:
- ➤ Hangtag: 4-5

If you're on a bear hunt, Curly is one of only five Beanies with nappy plush. Tan and curly, he comes equipped with a maroon ribbon around his neck.

Get the Scoop

Curly was used by Livent Productions as their Broadway Beanie for the show "Ragtime." He was sold with maroon, ivory, or navy ribbon, with "Ragtime" heat-stamped on the ribbon.

Erin the Bear

- ➤ Style: 4186
- ➤ Birthday: 3-17-97
- ➤ Released: 1-31-98
- ➤ Retired:
- ➤ Hangtag: 5

As bright kelly green as the rolling hills of Ireland itself, Erin the Irish bear comes equipped with an embroidered white shamrock on her chest—and no ribbon around her neck. If you're wanting your collection to be wearin' the green, better start looking for Erin today!

On the Sly

Part of the ever-popular new-faced bear group, Erin is harder to find than a four-leaf shamrock in a peat bog, so don't be surprised if she's difficult to find in stores for a long time to come.

Fortune the Panda

- ➤ Style: 4196
- ➤ Birthday: 12-6-97
- ➤ Released: 5-30-98
- ➤ Retired:
- ➤ Hangtag: 5

Fortune marks a whole new era in Beanie Baby bears, a completely different design from previous bears. Though a sit-up style, Fortune doesn't have the pouty nose of the other new-faced bears, nor the stitch under the chin that forms the nose. This black-and-white descendant of Peking the lay-down Panda also has a bright red ribbon around his neck.

On the Sly

Although Fortune has only just lumbered off the production line, counterfeit Fortunes have already turned up on the secondary market. So if you're seeking your Fortune, check him out closely!

Garcia the Bear

- ➤ Style: 4051
- ➤ Birthday: 8-1-95
- ➤ Released: 1-7-96
- ➤ Retired: 5-11-97
- ➤ Hangtag: 3-4

Garcia was created in honor of the late Jerry Garcia, from the rock band the Grateful Dead, with a combination of Jerry's birth month and day combined with the year of his death as Garcia's birthday. All you Beanie bear groupies can search out your own Garcia, the first of the new-faced bears to be released without a ribbon on his neck.

Get the Scoop

Garcia is unique, thanks to his tie-dye plush, so search out several and start your own rainbow collection!

Glory the Bear

- ➤ Style: 4188
- ➤ Birthday: 7-4-97
- ➤ Released: 5-30-98
- ➤ Retired:
- ➤ Hangtag: 5

Glory is the fourth Beanie to bear the Stars and Stripes. The others (Righty, Lefty, and Libearty) are all retired. Resplendent in white plush decorated with all-over red and blue stars and a fluttering Old Glory on his chest, expect him to be hard to find for quite a while due to his fairly recent release. Counterfeit Glorys can be found with a different poem.

Get the Scoop

The placement and size of the stars makes each individual Glory unique.

Libearty the Bear

- ➤ Style: 4057
- ➤ Birthday: Summer 1996
- ➤ Released: 6-15-96
- ➤ Retired: 1-1-97
- ➤ Hangtag: 4

The typographical error spelling Beanie as "Beanine" on Libearty's tush tag was one of the Beanie tag errors collectors consider a "classic." The version with the error is actually more common than the correct tag!

Get the Scoop

Libearty is the only Beanie whose birthday is a season (summer 1996) rather than a specific date. This is especially unusual since Libearty was one of the first releases with the fourth-generation hangtags, all of which come with birthdays.

Maple the Bear

- ➤ Style: 4600
- ➤ Birthday: 7-1-96
- ➤ Released: 1-1-97
- ➤ Retired:
- ➤ Hangtag: 4-5

Canadians may complain that their culture is overrun with goods, technology, and culture imported from the United States—but now the tide is turning with the introduction of this all-white, new-faced bear. Maple is highly sought after by Americans because he is sold exclusively in Canada, whose flag he wears proudly on his chest. Maple also wears a bright red ribbon around his neck. Be careful of that white plush!

Get the Scoop

Extremely rare (doubt it? check the price tag!) are versions with the name "Pride" on the tush tag rather than the correct name, "Maple."

Peace the Bear

- ➤ Style: 4053
- ➤ Birthday: 2-1-96
- ➤ Released: 5-11-97
- ➤ Retired:
- ➤ Hangtag: 4-5

Peace was given a chance once Garcia left the Beanie Baby stage and headed into retirement. The only difference between the two (other than the tags, of course) is the rainbow-colored peace symbol embroidered on Peace's chest. Even now, Peace can be very elusive in stores.

Get the Scoop

More recent shipments of Peace have a pastel tie-dye rather than the rainbow tie-dye that is so familiar; collectors still debate whether this is a temporary or permanent color change.

Peking the Panda

- ➤ Style: 4013
- ➤ Birthday: (none)
- ➤ Released: 6-25-94
- ➤ Retired: 1-7-96
- ➤ Hangtag: 1-3

There's no mistaking this black-and-white plush lay-down bear—he's all panda (the only thing missing are those bamboo shoots). Peking has black felt ovals through which his plastic eyes peer. Unfortunately, many of the Pekings on the market today are counterfeit.

On the Sly

There are three ways to spot a counterfeit Peking. First, they are generally a narrow shadow of the real thing (they have fewer pellets, making them very thin). Second, counterfeits have a much larger and more rounded black plastic nose. And third, the umlaut above the "ü" in "Nürnberg" is missing if he has a third-generation swing tag.

Princess the Bear

- ➤ Style: 4300
- ➤ Birthday: (none)
- ➤ Released: 10-29-97
- ➤ Retired:
- ➤ Hangtag: special

Born to the purple, the Princess bear is a Beanie of firsts, released to honor Diana, the Princess of Wales, after her tragic death in 1997. Princess is the only Beanie created after June 1996 who comes without a birthday. Her hangtag is printed in a special italic font, and Ty donates profits from her sale to Diana's Memorial Fund (more than $2 million so far). The beautiful deep-purple Princess has a white rose with green stem embroidered on her chest and wears a deep purple ribbon around her neck.

Get the Scoop

The Princess bear comes stuffed with one of two types of pellets; the PVC pellets are more valuable than the PE pellets.

Teddy the Bear (New-Faced)

- ➤ Style: 4050 (brown)
- ➤ Style: 4052 (cranberry)
- ➤ Style: 4057 (jade)
- ➤ Style: 4056 (magenta)
- ➤ Style: 4051 (teal)
- ➤ Style: 4055 (violet)
- ➤ Birthday: (none) (all colors except brown)
- ➤ Birthday: 11-28-95 (brown)
- ➤ Released: 1-7-95 (all colors)
- ➤ Retired: 1-7-96 (all colors except brown)
- ➤ Retired: 10-1-97 (brown)
- ➤ Hangtag: 2-3 (all colors except brown)
- ➤ Hangtag: 2-4 (brown)

The "new-faced" bears are the ones you're probably more familiar with, as it's the same style used on the current "sit-up" style of bears like Princess, Glory, and Erin. These bears all have a stitch under their chin that runs over the top of their snout and back down to help form their pouty-nosed look. Sometimes these stitches can break (or not be tied completely), giving the bears the look of an "old-faced" bear. However, it's easy to tell the difference: The new-faced bears' eyes are on the inside of the plush triangle that helps form their face, while the old-faced bears' eyes are on the outside.

Of all the colored bears, the only one not retired back in early 1996 was the NF Brown Teddy, who hung around until October 1997. Because we've been seeing so much of him, his retirement value is much less than those of the other colored NF bears.

If you find it's easier to unstick your nose from a honey jar than tell the difference between OFs and NFs, check this out: Each of the new-faced bears comes with a ribbon around its neck, something the old-faced bears don't have. Just to keep you from getting complacent, the mad seamstresses at Ty gave Cranberry a dark green ribbon and Jade a cranberry ribbon. (They make great Christmas season decorations with those color combinations!) Magenta's ribbon is pink, Teal's ribbon is navy blue, and Violet (the rarest NF bear) has a green ribbon.

Get the Scoop

When you read about Beanie bears, you may feel as if you're drowning in alphabet soup: You'll often see these bears referred to as NF (new face) or OF (old face). Many folks collect only one style or the other rather than both, especially because of their rarity and cost. The new-faced bears tend to be more popular.

Teddy the Bear (Old-Faced)

- ➤ Style: 4050 (brown)
- ➤ Style: 4052 (cranberry)
- ➤ Style: 4057 (jade)
- ➤ Style: 4056 (magenta)
- ➤ Style: 4051 (teal)
- ➤ Style: 4055 (violet)
- ➤ Birthday: (none) (all colors)
- ➤ Released: 6-25-94 (all colors)
- ➤ Retired: 1-7-95 (all colors)
- ➤ Hangtag: 1-2 (all colors)

You'll have to poke your way through quite a few caves before you uncover the old-faced brown bear, the rarest of any of the bears—old or new. Finding him in any condition is difficult at best, and if you find him you'll be faced with sticker shock: His price is generally several hundred to a thousand dollars more than the other old- or new-faced colored bears.

As you'd expect from their name, the OF bears are more Victorian in style, with pointier noses than those upstart pouty NF bears. Old-faced bears peer out of eyes set beyond the top triangle of plush that runs from their ears down to their noses.

The old-faced bears are plain, no-nonsense sort of bears, and don't go in for lots of fancy doodads like the decorative ribbons you'll see on the new-faced bears. If you notice a ribbon on an OF bear, be careful that it's just an add-on and not someone trying to pass off a counterfeit.

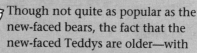

Get the Scoop
Though not quite as popular as the new-faced bears, the fact that the new-faced Teddys are older—with fewer survivors—helps keep their value closely in line with their younger cousins.

Teddy, 1997

- ➤ Style: 4200
- ➤ Birthday: 12-25-96
- ➤ Released: 10-1-97
- ➤ Retired: 12-31-97
- ➤ Hangtag: 4

The first in what appears to be Ty's decision to offer annual Beanies, the 1997 Teddy was not introduced until almost the end of the year. As a result, he was still arriving at stores when in fact he was retired, much to everyone's surprise. His value has bearly changed, but is expected to increase during the holiday season. His plush is lighter than the new-faced brown Teddy.

Get the Scoop

When originally introduced on the Ty Web site, the 1997 Teddy appeared in his publicity shots sporting red and green ribbons rather than a scarf. Actually, very few of these bears with ribbons are actually known to exist.

Valentino the Bear

- ➤ Style: 4058
- ➤ Birthday: 2-14-94
- ➤ Released: 1-7-95
- ➤ Retired:
- ➤ Hangtag: 2-5

Valentino is often the butt of retirement rumors, but the thing about retirement rumors is that sooner or later, they'll be right (and it will probably be sooner). Another of those hard-to-keep-clean white Beanies obviously related to Libearty and Maple, Valentino wears a red embroidered heart on his chest and a matching red ribbon around his neck.

Get the Scoop

If you're searching for that just-right Valentine's gift—or just a little something to let your sweetheart know how much you care—what could be better than a sweet Valentino bear?

It's a Jungle Out There

Some folks like to jet off to Kenya on safari to bag their prey. As far as I'm concerned, it's a heck of a lot cheaper (and easier on the wild animals) to go hunting for Beanie Baby jungle creatures instead. In fact, these critters are exotic enough for anyone's taste, and rare enough to pique the pride of any poacher.

Ants the Anteater

➤ Style: 4195
➤ Birthday: 11-7-97
➤ Released: 5-30-98
➤ Retired:
➤ Hangtag: 5

Ants is one of the May 30, 1998, releases and is generally considered to appeal to the kind of Beanie Baby fans who go for this type of creature in a big way. Odds are, if you like Tank, the retired armadillo, you'll love Ants. He's made of a light gray plush, and has a black plush stripe on his neck with white plush stripes on either side.

Get the Scoop

Ants has a real nose for his work; the size of his nose is surpassed only by his tail.

Bongo/Nana the Monkey

- ➤ Style: 4067
- ➤ Birthday: 8-17-95
- ➤ Released: 2-6-96 (brown-tailed)
- ➤ Released: 6-3-95 (tan-tailed)
- ➤ Retired: 6-29-96 (brown-tailed)
- ➤ Retired: (tan-tailed)
- ➤ Hangtag: 3-4 (brown-tailed)
- ➤ Hangtag: 3-5 (tan-tailed)

Bongo's first release went for the "total look," where his tan tail matched his face and paws. He was later released with a brown tail matching his body. Apparently the designers at Ty just couldn't make up their minds: Eventually, the tan-tailed version reappeared and now is valued more highly. Bongo is also found with the name Nana, a highly prized Beanie.

Get the Scoop

Not wanting to beat around the bush, marketing execs gave away 5,000 Bongos (together with a commemorative card) on April 5, 1998, at a Los Angeles Clippers–Cleveland Cavaliers basketball game.

Congo the Gorilla

- ➤ Style: 4160
- ➤ Birthday: 11-9-96
- ➤ Released: 6-15-96
- ➤ Retired:
- ➤ Hangtag: 4-5

Gentle Congo's black plush is offset by a brown face, ears, and paws. Unlike his buddy Bongo, Ty's designers haven't tampered with perfection: Congo hasn't undergone any design changes to date.

Get the Scoop

If you thought you'd noticed lots of giant Congos on store shelves, you could be right. Congo look-alikes (called "George") were created in various sizes for Ty's plush line.

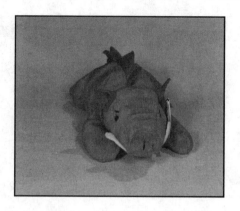

Grunt the Razorback

- ➤ Style: 4092
- ➤ Birthday: 7-19-95
- ➤ Released: 1-7-96
- ➤ Retired: 5-11-97
- ➤ Hangtag: 3-4

Often mistaken for Snort and Tabasco, Grunt will never be thought dull—his bright-red plush stands out at 50 paces, together with a fine set of white felt tusks (easily dirtied, alas), and a red felt spiky ridge along his back.

On the Sly

If you're rooting around for Grunt, beware! Counterfeit Grunts are thick on the ground. You know you've got a counterfeit if your Grunt has a more wrinkled appearance than the real thing.

Happy the Hippo

- ➤ Style: 4061
- ➤ Birthday: (none) (gray)
- ➤ Birthday: 2-25-94 (lavender)
- ➤ Released: 6-25-94 (gray)
- ➤ Released: 6-3-95 (lavender)
- ➤ Retired: 6-3-95 (gray)
- ➤ Retired: 5-1-98 (lavender)
- ➤ Hangtag: 1-3 (gray)
- ➤ Hangtag: 3-5 (lavender)

With a name sounding more like a flirtatious debutante than a fierce jungle creature, Happy was first released in light gray plush. Deciding that gray plush was on the drab side—not really happy enough for Happy—he was reformulated in a brighter lavender color that's sure to make anyone smile. We hope he's Happy in his retirement!

Get the Scoop

If you can find a gray Happy hippo, hang onto him. He's worth more than the lovely lavender shade.

Humphrey the Camel

- ➤ Style: 4060
- ➤ Birthday: (none)
- ➤ Released: 6-25-94
- ➤ Retired: 6-15-95
- ➤ Hangtag: 1-3

Perhaps the most beloved of the Beanies, Humphrey has floppy legs and a goofy plump face that make him almost irresistible. Elegant in a lighter, rich tan plush, he was put out to pasture for a well-earned retirement long ago.

Get the Scoop

Today, Humphrey is difficult to find. If you're lucky enough to get one, don't be surprised if he's missing his swing tag.

Peanut the Elephant

- ➤ Style: 4062
- ➤ Birthday: (none) (royal blue)
- ➤ Birthday: 1-25-95 (light blue)
- ➤ Released: 6-3-95 (royal blue)
- ➤ Released: 10-2-95 (light blue)
- ➤ Retired: 10-2-95 (royal blue)
- ➤ Retired: 5-1-98 (light blue)
- ➤ Hangtag: 3 (royal blue)
- ➤ Hangtag: 3-5 (light blue)

You'll never sing the blues if you've managed to snag one of these Peanuts dressed in royal blue! Possibly the most coveted of all Beanies, the blue fabric on Peanut is thought by many to have been a goof on the production line. The royal blue is the same color used on Kiwi's beak and in a section on Inch. Shortly after her release, Peanut was redesigned in a baby blue fabric. Both versions have pink plush on the inside of their ears.

Get the Scoop

All dressed up with no place to go, the newly-dyed light blue Peanut was part of an Oakland Athletics' giveaway on August 1, 1998.

Pouch the Kangaroo

➤ Style: 4161
➤ Birthday: 11-6-96
➤ Released: 1-1-97
➤ Retired:
➤ Hangtag: 4-5

Pouch is covered in brown plush except for her inner ears, chin, and stomach, which are off-white plush. She does have a pouch in there for stowing away her joey—but don't look too closely! Joey's actually a bodyless kangaroo with just a head! Joey is made of the same brown plush and has brown felt ears.

On the Sly

If you've tried to yank Pouch's baby out to get up close and personal, forget it! He's stitched into the pouch to help keep him safe.

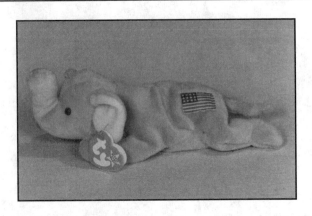

Righty the Elephant

➤ Style: 4085
➤ Birthday: 7-4-96
➤ Released: 6-15-96
➤ Retired: 1-1-97
➤ Hangtag: 4

Part of the American Trio (Righty, Lefty the donkey, and Libearty) released in the summer of 1996, Righty shares his birthday and his poem with Lefty. These are the only two Beanies brought out at the same time who share a poem, so these guys really are special.

Get the Scoop

Made of light gray plush with pink inner ears, Righty sports an American flag on his left hip. To have put it on his right side, where it should be politically, would make him politically incorrect (the stars would be too close to his hind end, considered an insult to the flag).

Spike the Rhinoceros

- ➤ Style: 4060
- ➤ Birthday: 8-13-96
- ➤ Released: 6-15-96
- ➤ Retired:
- ➤ Hangtag: 4-5

Short and stout, Spike has medium gray plush accented with a brown horn and inner ears. Until recently, Spike has been considered a "hard to find" Beanie, but has become more plentiful as shipments started coming to retailers regularly.

Get the Scoop

Will he be retired in the next Beanie wave? Will he remain current? Only Spike's creators know for sure!

Tank the Armadillo

- ➤ Style: 4031
- ➤ Birthday: (none) (7 lines, no shell)
- ➤ Birthday: 2-22-95 (9 lines, no shell)
- ➤ Birthday: 2-22-95 (shell)
- ➤ Released: 1-7-95 (7 lines, no shell)
- ➤ Released: circa 6-3-95 (9 lines, no shell)
- ➤ Released: (unknown) (shell)
- ➤ Retired: circa 1-7-96 (7 lines, no shell)
- ➤ Retired: (unknown) (9 lines, no shell)
- ➤ Retired: 10-1-97 (shell)
- ➤ Hangtag: 3 (7 lines, no shell)
- ➤ Hangtag: 4 (9 lines, no shell)
- ➤ Hangtag: 4 (shell)

You can count the number of lines on Tank to tell apart different varieties of him. The first two variations were longer than the final version, and both had embroidered nostrils. Finally, Ty seemed to understand that an armadillo should be armed with a shell and used a row of stitching along the bottom edge to form one. The last variation has a more rounded look to him and he has lost his nostrils. The 9-line, no shell variation is probably the rarest.

Get the Scoop

When counting Tank's lines, count the number of lines of stitching, not the number of lines between the stitching.

Twigs the Giraffe

- ➤ Style: 4068
- ➤ Birthday: 5-19-95
- ➤ Released: 1-7-96
- ➤ Retired: 5-1-98
- ➤ Hangtag: 3-5

If you thought you'd already spotted Twigs' orange-on-yellow spotted plush, you have—it also appears on the later version of Lizzy's stomach. Twigs' hooves are brown plush and he has a thin insert of brown plush as his mane.

Get the Scoop

Twigs' laid-back, sit-down body style was revisited in the May 1998 release of Whisper the deer.

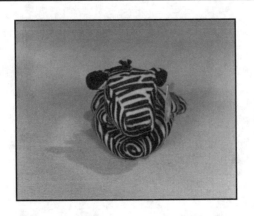

Ziggy the Zebra

- ➤ Style: 4063
- ➤ Birthday: 12-24-95
- ➤ Released: 6-3-95
- ➤ Retired: 5-1-98
- ➤ Hangtag: 5

Introduced in 1995 and retired three years later, Ziggy's plush coat was transformed from the less stylish narrow stripe to the far more fashionable wide-stripe look.

Get the Scoop

Ziggy has never appeared with a fine-yarn mane as have other Beanies.

Chapter 9

Wild and Wooly

In This Chapter

➤ Find two kinds of beavers: one-toothed and two-toothed

➤ Learn more about koalas: Are they bears or aren't they?

➤ Discover what woodland creature is the only current Beanie who was one of the Original Nine

While their counterparts in the jungle are more than fierce, woodland creatures have more guile than growl. All the critters you'd be likely to find in an American woods are corralled into this chapter, such as the fox, the deer, and the raccoon. The jungle hotheads are all contained in Chapter 8.

Bucky the Beaver

- ➤ Style: 4016
- ➤ Birthday: 6-8-95
- ➤ Released: 1-7-96
- ➤ Retired: 12-31-97
- ➤ Hangtag: 3-4

You'll be as busy as the proverbial you-know-what as you try to search out this little fellow. Bucky the beaver was created with body shape similar to Ringo, Sly, and Stinky. One of more than 30 Beanies colored mostly brown, he has darker brown ears and tail with an oval nose, whiskers, and felt teeth.

Get the Scoop

One tooth or two? Bucky inadvertently comes in both varieties: His teeth are made of one piece of felt, cut in the middle to make two teeth. However, sometimes the felt didn't get cut, leaving him with one huge tooth.

Chocolate the Moose

- ➤ Style: 4015
- ➤ Birthday: 4-27-93
- ➤ Released: 1-8-94
- ➤ Retired:
- ➤ Hangtag: 1-5

Chocolate is the only Beanie you can still find sitting on store shelves of the Original Nine. Looking good enough to eat in his chocolate brown plush (no surprise there), he's also got bright orange antlers. If you put him side-by-side with the ever-popular Humphrey the Camel, you'd see a fairly identical face.

Get the Scoop

Cartons of Chocolates (5,000 individual Chocolates) were given away as a sports promotion during the Denver Nuggets—Portland Trailblazers basketball game April 17, 1998.

Mel the Koala

- ➤ Style: 4162
- ➤ Birthday: 1-15-96
- ➤ Released: 1-1-97
- ➤ Retired:
- ➤ Hangtag: 4-5

Mel's plush is primarily medium-gray, though the insides of his ears and his stomach are white and his black plastic nose is rounder than the plastic noses you'll run across on other Beanies.

Get the Scoop

We would have filed Mel under "bears," except for the fact that koalas are really marsupials and not bears at all. Still, many people classify Mel as one of the Beanie bears.

Nuts the Squirrel

- ➤ Style: 4114
- ➤ Birthday: 1-21-96
- ➤ Released: 1-1-97
- ➤ Retired:
- ➤ Hangtag: 4-5

If you don't immediately fall in love with this little critter, then nuts to you! This Beanie Baby is popular because of the transmutation from plush to faux fur on his S-shaped tail. His brown plush matches his furry tail except for off-white plush on his stomach, chin, and the inner part of his ears.

Get the Scoop

Notice that your Nuts can sit up and beg without really trying? It's because he seems to be filled with more stuffing rather than "beans" in order to help keep him in his upright position.

Ringo the Raccoon

- ➤ Style: 4014
- ➤ Birthday: 7-14-95
- ➤ Released: 1-7-96
- ➤ Retired: 9-16-98
- ➤ Hangtag: 3-5

Primarily covered in brown plush, Ringo's tail is sewn vertically with black plush rings. His ears are black and white, and his snout is covered in white plush, with small areas of black plush around each eye to give him the masked look of real raccoons. His nose and whiskers are black.

Get the Scoop

You'll be running rings around your collector competition if you managed to snag a Ringo made with true-to-life gray-brown color before he retired in mid-September as part of the multiday retirement announcements.

Sly the Fox

➤ Style: 4115
➤ Birthday: 9-12-96
➤ Released: 6-15-96 (brown belly)
➤ Released: 8-6-96 (white belly)
➤ Retired: 8-6-96 (brown belly)
➤ Retired: 9-22-98 (white belly)
➤ Hangtag: 4 (brown belly)
➤ Hangtag: 4-5 (white belly)

The original brown-bellied version of Sly is possibly the most undervalued of all the Beanies even though he was only available for about two months. Perhaps in an attempt to make their Beanie fox more anatomically correct, the belly was changed to the white plush matching his chin and the inside of his ears.

Get the Scoop

Amazingly, the brown-bellied version of Sly still is reasonably priced (the $125 to $150 range), but I don't expect it to stay that way—especially now that Sly is retired.

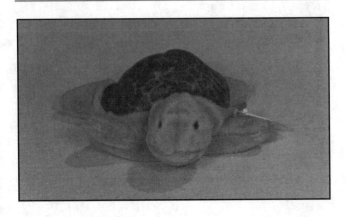

Speedy the Turtle

➤ Style: 4030
➤ Birthday: 8-14-94
➤ Released: 6-25-94
➤ Retired: 10-1-97
➤ Hangtag: 1-4

Speedy's body is lime green, the same color as Legs the frog. His shell is brown-on-green spotted like Slither's and Ally's backs. Even though he's been retired for a year, he's still easy to find at shows.

Get the Scoop

Except perhaps for youngsters with a penchant for all things reptilian, most collectors consider Speedy cute but not a Beanie with great emotional appeal.

Stinky the Skunk

➤ Style: 4017
➤ Birthday: 2-13-95
➤ Released: 6-3-95
➤ Retired: 9-28-98
➤ Hangtag: 3-5

Fortunately for collectors, Stinky doesn't live up to his odiferous name. Needless to say, he has black plush with a white stripe running from his nose to the tip of his tail.

Get the Scoop

He was around for quite a while (check out the fact that he's run through *all the* tush tags!) and therefore, he was fairly easy to find before, and probably will be after, his retirement.

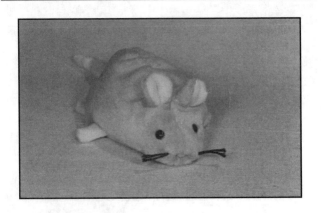

Trap the Mouse

➤ Style: 4042
➤ Birthday: (none)
➤ Released: 6-25-94
➤ Retired: 6-15-95
➤ Hangtag: 1-3

This light gray rodent with his pink plush feet, tail, and inner ears is one of the most popular of the older retired Beanies. Armed with sweet pink plastic nose and black (not pink!) whiskers, he fits easily into the palm of even the tiniest collector.

Get the Scoop

Taking bets on what animals will be released next, many collectors are hoping to trap a replacement for the dearly departed Trap.

Whisper the Deer

- ➤ Style: 4194
- ➤ Birthday: 4-5-97
- ➤ Released: 5-30-98
- ➤ Retired:
- ➤ Hangtag: 5

One of the last of the May 1998 releases, Whisper has a body style that is reminiscent of the late great Twigs the giraffe. Her brown plush is speckled with white spots along her back (indicating that she is still a young Beanie); her stomach and inner ears are white, but her hooves are brown.

Get the Scoop

Still hoofing it into the stores, she'll be hard to find for a while as every collector will want to add this "Bambi" look-alike to their herd.

Chapter 10

Still Life

In This Chapter

➤ Get some holiday and party decorating ideas with these Beanies

➤ Learn all about Magic's shades of thread and what they mean

➤ Get the scoop on Mystic's varieties: brown and shiny horns, fine and coarse manes

If your taste runs to the mystical and evanescent, this little group of non-living creatures—a small but captivating part of the Beanie Baby family—should be just your cup of Beanie tea. Even the scarier versions—ghosts and dragons—won't give the smallest child nightmares, so feel free to add all of these to your collection. In fact, some of the most beautiful creations of all the Beanies can be found here, with the hauntingly lovely, iridescent glimmer of a dragon's wing or a unicorn's horn. You'll also find the three versions of dinosaurs in this group—since dinosaurs are extinct, we felt they'd fit right in with the other "still life" group.

Bronty the Brontosaurus

- ➤ Style: 4085
- ➤ Birthday: (none)
- ➤ Released: 6-3-95
- ➤ Retired: 6-15-96
- ➤ Hangtag: 3

Bronty's plush is a deep blue tie-dye (the same as Sting's) with shades of light blue and green running through it. No two Brontys are exactly alike, since the material isn't a consistent color. He was released with dino pals Rex (a red tie-dye) and Steg, an earth-toned tie-dye.

Get the Scoop

Bronty is the rarest of the three dinosaurs, so try to add him to your collection before he becomes extinct!

Magic the Dragon

- ➤ Style: 4088
- ➤ Birthday: 6-8-95
- ➤ Released: 6-3-95
- ➤ Retired: 12-31-97
- ➤ Hangtag: 3-4

One of the two tallest Beanies, the all-white Magic is truly beautiful—and one of the most popular of all critters in the Ty collection. Magic's wings are crafted from an iridescent material and stuffed with filler (not beans) to help retain their shape. (Even dragons must bow to economic pressure; these wings were supposedly expensive for Ty to produce and were believed to be a factor in Magic's retirement.)

Get the Scoop

Originally, the stitching on Magic's wings and nostrils was a very light pink, giving way to a standard pink stitching with lighter pink nostrils. This evolved into a "hot pink" stitching with light pink nostrils. Most collectors believe that the hot pink stitching is the rarest, although some insist that the lightest pink is more valuable since it's found in the oldest dragons.

Mystic the Unicorn

- ➤ Style: 4007
- ➤ Birthday: (none) (fine mane)
- ➤ Birthday: 5-21-94 (brown horn)
- ➤ Birthday: 5-21-94 (iridescent horn)
- ➤ Released: 6-25-94 (fine mane)
- ➤ Released: (unknown) (brown horn)
- ➤ Released: 10-23-97 (iridescent horn)
- ➤ Retired: (unknown) (fine mane)
- ➤ Retired: 10-23-97 (brown horn)
- ➤ Retired: (iridescent horn)
- ➤ Hangtag: 1-3 (fine mane)
- ➤ Hangtag: 3-4 (brown horn)
- ➤ Hangtag: 4-5 (iridescent horn)

Here's another of those tough-to-keep-clean white Beanies. The original version of Mystic—like Derby the horse—had a mane and tail of fine yarn. Eventually, the fine yarn was replaced with coarser yarn, but both versions still had a stuffed gold felt horn. In the fall of 1997, however, Mystic's horn was transmuted into the same shiny material as Magic's wings, with a spiral of hot pink thread as an additional flourish. All three variations have blue eyes.

Get the Scoop

The fine-mane version of Mystic is easier to find than the fine-mane version of Derby, which is a real rarity.

Rex the Tyrannosaurus

- ➤ Style: 4086
- ➤ Birthday: (none)
- ➤ Released: 6-3-95
- ➤ Retired: 6-15-96
- ➤ Hangtag: 3

Released and retired before birthdays and poems were added to Beanie tags, Rex is the most popular of the dinosaur trio—Bronty, Rex, and Steg—and that's saying something, since all three of this group are real crowd-pleasers. Looking more colorful than a day-old bruise, Rex's tie-dyed plush varies from reds, pinks, and oranges all the way through purple, burgundy, and blue.

Get the Scoop

This little fellow's value is expected to soar, so try to find one in mint condition today for your collection.

Snowball the Snowman

- ➤ Style: 4201
- ➤ Birthday: 12-22-96
- ➤ Released: 10-1-97
- ➤ Retired: 12-31-97
- ➤ Hangtag: 4

Released and retired quicker than a snowball melts in spring, Snowball was the second "non-animal" Beanie ever produced. (The first was Spooky the ghost.) Snowball sports a jaunty black felt hat with a red band, a red scarf with white fringe, orange felt for his carrot nose, and black plastic bits of "coal" for his eyes. He's a favorite choice for holiday winter party decorations, which is one reason why he was popular.

Get the Scoop

Snowball's early retirement came as a surprise to collectors. Expect his value to snowball during the holiday season!

Spooky the Ghost

➤ Style: 4090
➤ Birthday: 10-31-95
➤ Released: 9-1-95
➤ Retired: 12-31-97
➤ Hangtag: 3-4

Until Snowball came along and shoved him out of the limelight, Spooky had the distinction of being Ty's only non-living Beanie Baby. However, both of these creatures were retired in 1997, leaving only animals in the Ty company stable. Spooky was unique in another way: He's the only Beanie whose designer (Jenna Boldebeck) was listed in the third-generation hangtag. These same third-generation tags also mistakenly call him "Spook" (but it's not certain whether someone hit the wrong key on the computer, or whether this was an intentional renaming). As usual, Ty's not talking.

On the Sly

Don't get spooked if you notice that your Spooky's mouth looks different than somebody else's. Spooky's mouth correctly comes in several different configurations.

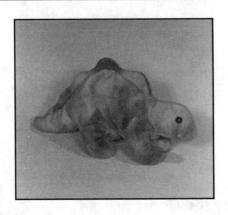

Steg the Stegosaurus

- ➤ Style: 4087
- ➤ Birthday: (none)
- ➤ Released: 6-3-95
- ➤ Retired: 6-15-96
- ➤ Hangtag: 3

The last of the dino trio to be released, Steg is covered in tie-dye plush in mostly earth tones of yellow, tan, and green. The muted colors tend to make him less popular than his chums Bronty and Rex, but he's still got that unmistakable Beanie charm.

Get the Scoop

While he might not win any beauty contests, Steg was never released in Europe and is considered to be rarer than his cousin Rex.

Chapter 11

A Teenie Tribute

In This Chapter

➤ Learn how Ty and McDonald's collaborated on the most popular McDonald's promotion ever held.

➤ Get the scoop on the worth of a complete set of Teenie Beanies

➤ Find out when the next McDonald's promotion may occur

When a company like Ty gets together with a company like McDonald's—both known for their marketing wizardry—you can expect something amazing to happen, and that's just what occurred on April 11, 1997, when the Teenie Beanie promotion began.

The First Set of Teenie Beanie Babies

The deal: McDonald's would give away one of 10 different styles of miniature versions of Ty's Beanie Babies (called "Teenie Beanies") with each purchase of a Happy Meal at participating restaurants. The Teenie Beanies were licensed by Ty, but produced by an independent McDonald's supplier. When news leaked out that the Teenie Beanies had arrived, McDonalds' employees were stunned by the pandemonium that followed. Once the dust had settled, hundreds of thousands of new Beanie Baby collectors were born—and McDonald's was forced to run national TV ads apologizing to customers for running out of the furry little creatures. In less than two weeks, more than 100,000 Teenie Beanies were distributed in the promotion, which was termed the most successful McDonald's promotion ever devised.

After each McDonald's received the first set of 10 teenie Beanies, many restaurants found they had used up their entire supply, that should have lasted for a week, within a day or two.

1997 Teenie Beanie set #1.

Chocolate the Moose

- ➤ Number in set: 4
- ➤ Released: April 1997
- ➤ Retired: April 1997

Get the Scoop

The next official date for the McDonald's Teenie Beanie promotion is scheduled for April 23, 1999, according to *Advertising Age* magazine.

Chops the Lamb

- ➤ Number in set: 3
- ➤ Released: April 1997
- ➤ Retired: April 1997

Baby Talk

The letters **TBB** stand for Teenie Beanie Baby.

Goldie the Fish

- ➤ Number in set: 3
- ➤ Released: April 1997
- ➤ Retired: April 1997

Lizz the Lizard

- ➤ Number in set: 10
- ➤ Released: April 1997
- ➤ Retired: April 1997

Baby Talk

The abbreviation **HTF** is used among collectors to mean "hard to find."

Patti the Platypus

- ➤ Number in set: 1
- ➤ Released: April 1997
- ➤ Retired: April 1997

Get the Scoop

Teenie Patti is almost as rare as Pinky. If you've got a mint-in-the-bag Patti, she's worth between $30 and $35.

Pinky the Flamingo

- ➤ Number in set: 2
- ➤ Released: April 1997
- ➤ Retired: April 1997

Get the Scoop

Pinky is the rarest TBB from the first set (worth about $40 if she's mint and still in her package).

Quacks the Duck

➤ Number in set: 9
➤ Released: April 1997
➤ Retired: April 1997

Get the Scoop

Quacks the duck (and Lizz the lizard) are the only Teenie Beanies from the first set to not use the same name as their larger "Moms" or "Dads."

Seamore the Seal

➤ Number in set: 7
➤ Released: April 1997
➤ Retired: April 1997

Get the Scoop

While the Teenies originally were offered free with a McDonald's Happy Meal, today a complete set in the original packages sells for about $75 or more.

Snort the Bull
- ➤ Number in set: 8
- ➤ Released: April 1997
- ➤ Retired: April 1997

Get the Scoop

The home offices of both Ty, Inc., and McDonald's are located in Oak Brook, Illinois.

Speedy the Turtle
- ➤ Number in set: 6
- ➤ Released: April 1997
- ➤ Retired: April 1997

Get the Scoop

Rumors suggest that McDonalds had 10 million of each Teenie Baby produced, for a total of 100 million Teenies.

The Second Set of Teenie Beanie Babies

The first promotion was so popular, a second McDonald's Teenie Beanie giveaway was scheduled May 22, 1998, as part of a Memorial Day weekend promotion. This time, 12 teenie-tiny Teenie Beanies (again licensed by Ty, but produced by an independent McDonald's supplier) were included in the promotional offerings. It was up to the individual stores to decide how many would be offered at one

1998 Teenie Beanie set #2.

time. Some stores offered one, some offered two—and some offered all 12 at once.

Customers could see which toys were available at any one time by reading posters in the windows of the store, or checking out the signs in the drive-through lane. Rumor has it that there were 240 million produced.

Interestingly, if you're into collecting, remember that it might not be a good idea to toss that Happy Meal bag away while you're grappling for the Teenie Beanie inside. Even the Happy Meal bag the TBBs came in is being traded on the secondary market. Some Teenie Beanie bag trivia:

➤ Some areas got Happy Meal boxes, not bags.

➤ There are two different styles of Teenie Beanie Baby bags for the second set.

➤ Happy meal bags may sell for between $1 and $5.

➤ In the second promotional set, some of the Teenie plastic bags are printed in three languages (English, French and Spanish)—later shipments added German.

Bones the Dog
- ➤ Number in set: 9
- ➤ Released: May 1998
- ➤ Retired: May 1998

Get the Scoop

In the second McDonald's promotion, three different Beanies were offered at one time, but while the promotion was intended to last for a month, once again the incredible Beanie frenzy depleted supplies within a few days.

Bongo the Monkey
- ➤ Number in set: 2
- ➤ Released: May 1998
- ➤ Retired: May 1998

Doby the Doberman
- ➤ Number in set: 1
- ➤ Released: May 1998
- ➤ Retired: May 1998

Get the Scoop

While the Teenie Beanies were included free as part of the McDonald's Happy Meal, consumers also could buy a toy for about $1.50 (depending on the store) if they also purchased one meal item.

Happy the Hippo

➤ Number in set: 6
➤ Released: May 1998
➤ Retired: May 1998

Baby Talk

A Beanie that is the most recent is called a **new release**. Beanies referred to as **current** are those easily found at local stores.

Inch the Inchworm

➤ Number in set: 4
➤ Released: May 1998
➤ Retired: May 1998

Mel the Koala

➤ Number in set: 7
➤ Released: May 1998
➤ Retired: May 1998

Baby Talk

The abbreviation **MIB** stands for "Mint In Bag," meaning that the Beanie is in mint condition and comes in its original bag.

Peanut the Elephant

- ➤ Number in set: 12
- ➤ Released: May 1998
- ➤ Retired: May 1998

Pinchers the Lobster

- ➤ Number in set: 5
- ➤ Released: May 1998
- ➤ Retired: May 1998

Get the Scoop

McDonald's produced a mass of Teenie Beanie accessories in 1998 for their employees, such as a group of enameled lapel pins.

Scoop the Pelican

- ➤ Number in set: 8
- ➤ Released: May 1998
- ➤ Retired: May 1998

Get the Scoop

The original McDonald's Teenie Beanie promotion was slated to have lasted for five weeks, but it was so popular—causing hour-long lines at the drive-through windows across the country—that all the 100,000 Teenie Beanies had been given out within a week or so.

Twigs the Giraffe

- ➤ Number in set: 3
- ➤ Released: May 1998
- ➤ Retired: May 1998

Get the Scoop

Twigs is rumored to be the most rare in the second set due to a manufacturing error that rendered about half the production run unusable.

Waddle the Penguin

- ➤ Number in set: 11
- ➤ Released: May 1998
- ➤ Retired: May 1998

Get the Scoop

The complete set from the first promotion is worth between $150 and $200; the second set is worth between $50 and $75. If you've already ripped open the package to play with your Teenie Beanie, too bad for you. Out of the bags, the first set is worth about $50 and the second, about $20.

Zip the Cat

- ➤ Number in set: 10
- ➤ Released: May 1998
- ➤ Retired: May 1998

Further Reading

Beanie Magazines

Beanie Collector
Published bi-monthly.
Beckett & Associates, publisher

Beanie Mania
Published bi-monthly.
Beanie Mania LLC, publisher

Beans!
Published monthly.
Tuff Stuff Publications

Mary Beth's Beanie World
Published monthly.
H & S Media, publisher

Mary Beth's Beanie World for Kids
Published quarterly.
H & S Media, publisher

Beanie Books

Brecka, Shawn. *The Bean Family Album*. Norfolk, VA: Antique Trader Books, 1998.

_____. *The Bean Family Pocket Guide*. Norfolk, VA: Antique Trader Books, 1998.

Carey, Susan S. and Ryan M. Carey. *The Beanie Encyclopedia: Identification and Values*. Paducah, KY: Collector Books, 1998.

Cook, Rachel, et.al. *Encyclo-Beanie-A: An Educational Reference Guide to Beanie Babies & the Animal Kingdom*. Seattle, WA: Buckaroo Books, 1998.

Fox, Les and Sue Fox. *The Beanie Baby Handbook: Fall 1998*. Midland Park, NJ: West Highland Publishing Co., 1998.

Neebascher, B. *The Official Beanie Basher Handbook*. Kansas City, MO: Andrews & McMeel, 1998.

Phillips, Becky and Becky Estenssoro. *Beanie Mania: A Comprehensive Collector's Guide*. Naperville, IL: Dinomates, Inc., 1997.

_____. *Beanie Mania II: A Comprehensive Collector's Guide*. Naperville, IL: Dinomates, Inc., 1998.

_____. *Beanie Mania II With Poster*. Naperville, IL: Dinomates, Inc., 1998.

_____. *Beanie Mania International*. Naperville, IL: Dinomates, Inc., 1998.

Stowe, Holly. *Beanie Babies Collector's Guide*. New York, NY: Penguin USA, 1998.

Wells, Rosie (ed). *Rosie's Price Guide for Ty's Beanie Babies*. Canton, IL: Rosie Wells Enterprises, Inc., 1998.

_____. *Beanie Digest*. Canton, IL: Rosie Wells Enterprises, Inc., 1998.

Beanie Web Sites

News, articles, and references to other links:

Ty, Inc.
www.ty.com

BeanieMom
www.beaniemom.com

Ctoys
www.ctoys.com

Beaniemonium
www.beaniemonium.com

Mary Beth's Beanie World
www.beanieworld.net

Beanie Mania LLC
www.beaniemania.net

The Beanie Philes
www.beaniephiles.com

Beanieholics
www.geocities.com/Heartland/Park/4116/

RJW Retail (Canada)
www.beaniemania.com

Ashley's Awesome Beanies
www.awesomebeanies.com

The Toy Box
www.the-toybox.com

Beanie Phenomenon
www.beaniephenomenon.com/

Janie Davis
www.netreach.net/people/rjones/beanie.html

K 'n K Collectibles
www.knkcollectibles.com

Swap meets and shows:

www.beaniemom.com/swaplinks.html

Pricing guides:

www.beaniemom.com/beaninfo.html

www.beaniephenomenon.com/checklist.html

www.ctoys.com/list/

Merchants links:

www.beaniemom.com/mercmain.html

www.beaniemania.com/ring/ring.html

Auctions, classifieds, and trading boards:

www.beaniemom.com/collcorn.html

cgi.ty.com/fastcgi/viewguest.fcgi

toys.ebay.com

up4sale.com/beaniebabies.html

jango.excite.com/xsh/
query.dcg?cat=beanies&svc=&cobrand=xsh

Counterfeit info:

www.beaniemom.com/countermain.html

Links for accessories:

www.beaniemom.com/accessmain.html

http://www.netreach.net/people/rjones/
beanie.html#Accessories

Beanbag-toy–related books:

www.amazon.com

www.barnesandnoble.com

www.borders.com

Beanie Babies— Approximate Market Values

Values approximated for October 15, 1998; retireds as of September 27, 1998. Currents valued $5–7 US, $8–15 Cdn, 10–15 pounds sterling.

Ally the alligator	$38–45
Ants the anteater	$5–7
Baldy the eagle	$11–15
Batty the bat	$5–7
Bernie the St. Bernard	$9–12
Bessie the cow	$55–62
Blackie the bear	$9–12
Blizzard the tiger	$11–15
Bones the dog	$11–15
Bongo (brown tail)	$48–55
Bongo (tan tail)	$5–7
Britannia the bear	10–15 pounds sterling
Bronty the brontosaurus	$800–950

Brownie the bear	$2,800–3,200
Bruno the terrier	$10–14
Bubbles the fish	$100–115
Bucky the beaver	$32–38
Bumble the bee	$475–525
Caw the crow	$500–550
Chilly the polar bear	$1,800–2,000
Chip the cat	$5–7
Chocolate the moose	$5–7
Chops the lamb	$135–160
Claude the crab	$5–7
Congo the gorilla	$5–7
Coral the fish	$160–175
Crunch the shark	$5–7
Cubbie the bear	$20–25
Curly the bear	$5–7
Daisy the cow	$9–12
Derby the horse (fine mane)	$2,750–3,250
Derby the horse (coarse mane)	$20–25
Derby the horse (star)	$5–7
Digger the orange crab	$700–800
Digger the red crab	$90–100
Doby the Doberman	$5–7
Doodle the rooster	$35–40
Dotty the Dalmatian	$5–7

Early the robin	$5–7
Ears the brown rabbit	$11–15
Echo the dolphin	$11–15
Erin the bear	$5–7
Fetch the Golden Retriever	$5–7
Flash the dolphin	$90–100
Fleece the lamb	$5–7
Flip the white cat	$30–35
Floppity the lilac bunny	$11–15
Flutter the butterfly	$900–1,000
Fortune the panda	$5–7
Freckles the leopard	$5–7
Garcia the bear	$140–160
Gigi the Poodle	$5–7
Glory the bear	$5–7
Gobbles the turkey	$5–7
Goldie the goldfish	$32–38
Gracie the swan	$11–15
Grunt the razorback	$140–160
Happy the gray hippo	$625–725
Happy the lavender hippo	$11–15
Hippity the mint bunny	$11–15
Hissy the snake	$5–7
Hoot the owl	$32–40
Hoppity the rose bunny	$11–15

Humphrey the camel	$1,600–1,850
Iggy the iguana (bright tie-dye, no tongue)	$10–15
Iggy the iguana (bright tie-dye, tongue)	$12–17
Iggy the iguana (blue tie-dye)	$5–7
Inch the inchworm (felt antennae)	$135–160
Inch the inchworm (yarn antennae)	$12–18
Inky the octopus (tan—mouth)	$650–750
Inky the octopus (tan—no mouth)	$750–850
Inky the pink octopus	$15–20
Jabber the parrot	$5–7
Jake the mallard duck	$5–7
Jolly the walrus	$11–15
Kiwi the toucan	$160–180
Kuku the cockatoo	$5–7
Lefty the donkey	$250–300
Legs the frog	$15–22
Libearty the bear	$325–375
Lizzy the blue lizard	$22–27
Lizzy the tie-dyed lizard	$900–1,000
Lucky the ladybug (11 spots)	$18–22
Lucky the ladybug (21 spots)	$500–600
Lucky the ladybug (7 spots)	$160–180
Magic the dragon	$40–50
Manny the manatee	$150–175
Maple the bear	$8–15 Cdn

Mel the koala	$5–7
Mystic the unicorn (fine mane)	$200–250
Mystic the unicorn (brown horn)	$28–35
Mystic the unicorn (iridescent horn)	$5–7
Nana the tan-tailed monkey	$3,500–4,000
Nanook the Husky	$5–7
Nip the gold cat	$850–900
Nip the gold cat (white face)	$500–550
Nip the gold cat (white paws)	$18–22
Nuts the squirrel	$5–7
Patti the fuchsia platypus	$15–20
Patti the maroon platypus	$700–1,000
Peace the bear	$5–7
Peanut the light blue elephant	$11–15
Peanut the royal blue elephant	$4,500–5,000
Peking the panda	$1,800–2,000
Pinchers the lobster	$11–15
Pinky the flamingo	$5–7
Pouch the kangaroo	$5–7
Pounce the cat	$5–7
Prance the cat	$5–7
Princess the bear	$5–7
Puffer the puffin	$10–14
Pugsly the Pug dog	$5–7
Punchers the lobster	$2,800–3,200

Quackers the duck (with wings)	$11–15
Quackers the duck (wingless)	$1,750–2,000
Radar the bat	$130–160
Rainbow the chameleon (blue tie-dye)	$10–15
Rainbow the chameleon (bright tie-dye)	$5–7
Rex the tyrannosaurus	$800–950
Righty the elephant	$250–300
Ringo the raccoon	$8–12
Roary the lion	$5–7
Rocket the blue jay	$5–7
Rover the dog	$15–20
Scoop the pelican	$5–7
Scottie the Scottish Terrier	$18–22
Seamore the seal	$125–150
Seaweed the otter	$15–20
Slither the snake	$1,800–2,000
Sly the brown-bellied fox	$125–150
Sly the white-bellied fox	$5–7
Smoochy the frog	$5–7
Snip the Siamese cat	$5–7
Snort the bull	$8–12
Snowball the snowman	$38–45
Sparky the Dalmatian	$100–125
Speedy the turtle	$28–35
Spike the rhinoceros	$5–7

Spinner the spider	$9–14
Splash the whale	$90–100
Spooky the ghost	$28–38
Spot the dog with a spot	$38–45
Spot the dog without a spot	$1,800–2,000
Spunky the Cocker Spaniel	$5–7
Squealer the pig	$20–25
Steg the stegosaurus	$800–900
Sting the stingray	$150–175
Stinger the scorpion	$5–7
Stinky the skunk	$8–12
Stretch the ostrich	$5–7
Stripes the tiger (dark)	$275–325
Stripes the tiger (light)	$11–15
Strut the rooster	$5–7
Tabasco the bull	$150–175
Tank the armadillo (7 lines without shell)	$165–180
Tank the armadillo (9 lines without shell)	$175–200
Tank the armadillo (with shell)	$60–70
Teddy the new-faced brown bear	$70–90
Teddy the new-faced cranberry bear	$1,750–1,950
Teddy the new-faced jade bear	$1,750–1,950
Teddy the new-faced magenta bear	$1,750–1,950
Teddy the new-faced teal bear	$1,750–1,950
Teddy the new-faced violet bear	$1,750–1,950

Teddy the old-faced brown bear	$2,750–3,250
Teddy the old-faced cranberry bear	$1,750–1,950
Teddy the old-faced jade bear	$1,750–1,950
Teddy the old-faced magenta bear	$1,750–1,950
Teddy the old-faced teal bear	$1,750–1,950
Teddy the old-faced violet bear	$1,750–1,950
Teddy, 1997	$40–60
Tracker the Bassett Hound	$5–7
Trap the mouse	$1,250–1,500
Tuffy the terrier	$5–7
Tusk the walrus	$120–140
Twigs the giraffe	$12–18
Valentino the bear	$5–7
Velvet the panther	$22–30
Waddle the penguin	$11–15
Waves the whale	$11–15
Web the spider	$1,250–1,500
Weenie the Dachshund	$18–25
Whisper the deer	$5–7
Wise the owl	$5–7
Wrinkles the Bulldog	$8–12
Ziggy the zebra	$15–20
Zip the all-black cat	$1,650–1,800
Zip the black cat (white face)	$625–675
Zip the black cat (white paws)	$32–40

Index

S

News Flash!

As this book was going to press, Ty announced 10 new Beanie Babies along with a new product line of larger Beanie-look-alikes called "Beanie Buddies"! Permit me to introduce you to the latest Beanie Babies!

Beak   Well, I'm having a tough time deciding whether Beak is a kiwi bird or an emu. His (her?) beak is much more kiwi-like than emu-ish, but kiwis only have the most rudimentary of wings. Beak's are more pronounced. His/her fur appears to be yet another new kind of plush, a longer napped fur. I can't wait to see Beak in person!

Canyon   Cougar is the best guess for this feline. It's light brown in color with ear fronts of white plush and backs of black plush. Its belly and snout are white plush, and the white plush on its snout is surrounded by a thin line of black plush. Purrrr-fect!

Halo   A white new-faced bear, Halo bears what looks like the retired Magic's wings of iridescent material filled with stuffing. S/he also has, what else, a halo made of the same material. Collectors will be dancing rings around this bear.

Loosy   Goosey! Joining Jake the mallard drake, Loosy is similar in style and coloring, but with the black head and white "chin strap" of the Canadian goose. Loosy also sports a red bow around his neck. You may have to migrate to find this bird in the stores anytime soon!

Pumkin   Only the third "thing" Beanie, following in the footsteps of Spooky and Snowball. Pumkin is a pumpkin, of course! This pumpkin has a topknot of dark green plush leaves and long, viney arms and legs. Not nearly as scary as the recently departed Halloween spider, Spinner.

Roam Oh, give me a home for the buffalo, Roam! I've got to admit, of the non-holiday Beanies, Roam is probably going to be my favorite with his nappy fur on his head, shoulders, and front legs and smooth plush on his hindquarters. (Not to mention the little bit of nappy plush at the tip of his tail!)

Santa A Beanie first—a "person" Beanie! Santa is... well... Santa! Complete with white, fluffy beard and Santa hat (one of three Beanies in this release with Santa-type caps!), the most distinguishing (and surprising) feature is Santa's Erin-green mittens! (Or maybe Santa is really Legs in disguise.)

Scorch It took me a minute upon looking at the name of this new Beanie to realize what it was. It's a new dragon to replace our dearly departed Magic. Very similar in shape and size to the all-white Magic, Scorch appears to be the love child of Pounce and Fleece with what seems to be brown tie-dye nappy plush. His wings are iridescent gold, and is that a tongue or a little flame shooting from his mouth?

Zero Think of Waddle, then put a Santa cap on him and you have Zero. It's hard to tell at this point if Zero is supposed to be a holiday Beanie (and perhaps intended to be short-lived) or just a winter Beanie. If you can find him in the store, check out his poem to see what you think!

1998 Holiday Teddy All it takes is a glance at my given name to figure out which Beanie is my favorite among this set of new releases. If you replace the stars on Glory with holly leaves and holly berries, then stick a Santa-style cap (of the same plush) on her, add green and red ribbons around her neck (like the original pictures and rare version of the 1997 Teddy), and you'll have my "berry" favorite bear!